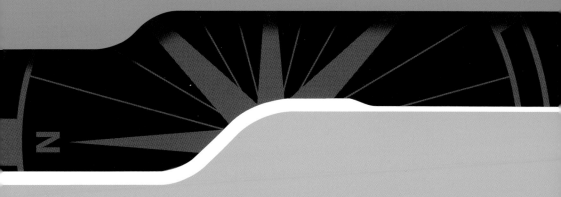

curriculum
connections

Atlas of World History

The Middle Ages
600–1492

BROWN
BEAR
BOOKS

Published by Brown Bear Books Limited

An imprint of:
The Brown Reference Group Ltd
68 Topstone Road
Redding
Connecticut 06896
USA
www.brownreference.com

ISBN: 978-1-933834-67-2

Editorial Director: Lindsey Lowe
Senior Managing Editor: Tim Cooke
Managing Editor: Rachel Tisdale
Editor: Helen Dwyer
Designer: Barry Dwyer

**Library of Congress Cataloging-in-Publication
Data available upon request**

Picture Credits

Cover Image
Shutterstock: Stefan Ataman

Artwork © The Brown Reference Group Ltd

The Brown Reference Group Ltd has made
every effort to trace copyright holders of the
pictures used in this book. Anyone having
claims to ownership not identified above is
invited to contact The Brown Reference
Group Ltd.

Printed in the United States of America

Contents

Introduction

Atlas of World History forms part of the Curriculum Connections series. The six volumes of this set cover all the major periods of the World History curriculum: The First Civilizations (4,000,000–500 BCE); The Classical World (500 BCE–600 CE); The Middle Ages (600–1492); The Early Modern World (1492–1783); Industrialization and Empire (1783–1914); and World Wars and Globalization (1914–2010).

About this set

Each volume in *Atlas of World History* features thematic world and regional maps. All of the regional maps are followed by an in-depth article.

The volume opens with a series of maps that provide an overview of the world at particular dates. They show at-a-glance how the shape of the world changed during the period covered in the book. The rest of the volume is divided into regional sections, each of which covers a continent or part of a continent. Within each section, maps appear in broadly chronological order. Each map highlights a particular period or topic, which the accompanying article explains in a concise but accurate summary.

Within each article, two key aids to learning are located in sidebars in the margins of each page:

Curriculum Context sidebars indicate that a subject has particular relevance to certain key state and national World and American history guidelines and curricula. They highlight essential information or suggest useful ways for students to consider a subject or to include it in their studies.

Glossary sidebars define key words within the text.

At the end of the book, a summary Glossary lists the key terms defined in the volume. There is also a list of further print and Web-based resources and a full volume index.

About this book

The Middle Ages is a fascinating guide to the history of humankind from the emergence of Islam as a major religion to the epochal voyages of Christopher Columbus.

The volume begins with a series of maps that present an overview of the grand themes of history at key dates between 600 and 1492. The maps chart the shifting pattern of human settlement and the rise and fall of empires and states, in addition to reviewing the spread of trade and exploration on a world scale.

The regional maps that follow look more closely at the great events of the period: the flowering of medieval Europe and the Renaissance, the far-flung Islamic empire of the Arabs, Tang and Song China, and the dynamic Mongol and Inca empires. There is also coverage of less familiar histories, such as those of medieval Japan, the empire of Harsha in India, the first African empires, and the Thai state of Nan Chao.

TYPOGRAPHICAL CONVENTIONS	
World maps	
FRANCE	state or empire
Belgian Congo	dependency or territory
Mongols	tribe, chiefdom or people
Anasazi culture	cultural group
Regional maps	
HUNGARY	state or empire
Bohemia	dependency or territory
Slavs	tribe, chiefdom or people
ANATOLIA	geographical region
✕	battle
•	site or town

The World in 800 CE

By 800, the classical world had broken up and an Islamic empire
had spread rapidly in West Asia. Both China and India were home
to significant empires, but while western Europe was unified
under the Carolingians, the continent's fringes remained
fragmented. The Americas and Africa were dominated by
hunter–gatherers, although both continents were also home
to regions of sometimes highly developed urban culture.

N

Greenland

Iceland

Arctic marine mammal hunters

Aleuts

sub-Arctic forest hunter-gatherers

plateau fishers and
hunter-gatherers

west coast foraging,
hunting and fishing
peoples

desert hunter-
gatherers

eastern woodlands
hunter-gatherers
and cultivators

Celtic
kingdoms

Anglo–Saxon
kingdoms

CAROLIN
EMPI

Anasazi
culture

plains bison
hunters

Mississippian
temple-mound
builders

ASTURIAS

UMAYYAD
CALIPHATE

Lomb
duc

Hohokam
culture

Mogollon
culture

desert hunter-
gatherers

IDRISID CALIPHATE

AGHLABII
EMIRAT

Hawaiian
Islands

maize
farmers

TOLTEC
EMPIRE

Bahamas

Cuba

Carib farmers

camel

Mesoamerican
city-states

Maya
city-states

Hispaniola

GHANA

MONTE ALBÁN
(Zapotecs)

west African ch

north Andean
chiefdoms

Amazonian
chiefdoms

Polynesians

manioc farmers

HUARI EMPIRE

savanna
hunter-gatherers

farming replacing
hunter-gathering

TIAHUANACO
EMPIRE

pampas
hunter-gatherers

shellfish gatherers and
marine mammal hunters

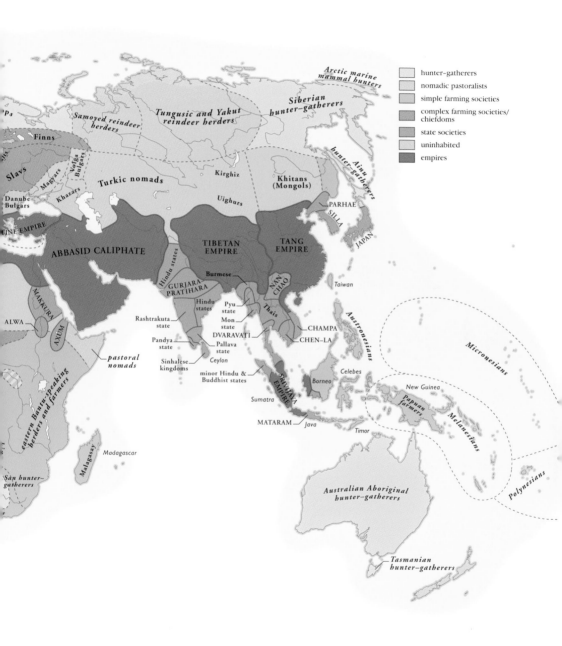

Arctic marine
mammal hunters

hunter-gatherers
nomadic pastoralists
simple farming societies
complex farming societies/
chiefdoms
state societies
uninhabited
empires

Siberian
hunter-gatherers

Tungusic and Yakut
reindeer herders

Samoyed reindeer
herders

Ps

Finns

Slavs

Magyars

Volga
Bulgars

Danube
Bulgars

Khazars

Turkic nomads

Kirghiz

Khitans
(Mongols)

hunter-Ainu gatherers

Uighurs

PARHAE

SILLA

BYZANTINE EMPIRE

JAPAN

ABBASID CALIPHATE

TIBETAN
EMPIRE

TANG
EMPIRE

Hindu states

Burmese

NAN
CHAO

Taiwan

Austronesians

GURJARA
PRATIHARA

Hindu
states

Pyu
state

Thais

Micronesians

Rashtrakuta
state

Mon
state

DVARAVATI

CHAMPA

CHEN–LA

MAKKURA

ALWA

AXUM

Pandya
state

Pallava
state

Celebes

New Guinea

pastoral
nomads

Sinhalese
kingdoms

Ceylon

Borneo

Papuan
farmers

Melanesians

eastern Bantu-speaking
herders and farmers

minor Hindu &
Buddhist states

SRIVIJAYA
EMPIRE

Sumatra

MATARAM

Java

Timor

San hunter-
gatherers

Malagasy

Madagascar

Australian Aboriginal
hunter-gatherers

Polynesians

Tasmanian
hunter-gatherers

The World in 1000

By 1000, stable states and kingdoms were emerging in Europe, where the Holy Roman empire had been established. At the same time as the Arab world continued to fragment into small states, the Islamic world expanded. The Chinese empire had shrunk, and the Khmer had become the greatest power in southeast Asia. In North America, farming communities and large settlements had developed in the eastern woodlands, the southwestern deserts, and the Mississippi area.

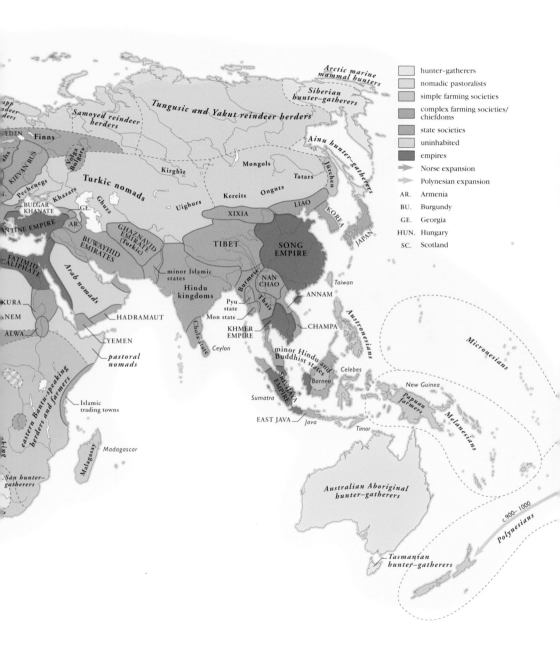

hunter-gatherers
nomadic pastoralists
simple farming societies
complex farming societies/
chiefdoms
state societies
uninhabited
empires
Norse expansion
Polynesian expansion
AR.   Armenia
BU.   Burgundy
GE.   Georgia
HUN. Hungary
SC.   Scotland

*Arctic marine
mammal hunters*

*Siberian
hunter-gatherers*

Tungusic and Yakut reindeer herders

*Samoyed reindeer
herders*

Ainu hunter-gatherers

EDEN   Finns

Volga
Bulgars

KIEVAN RUS

Kirghiz

Mongols

Tatars

Jurchen

Pechenegs

Khazars

Turkic nomads

Kereits

Onguts

LIAO

KOREA

BULGAR
KHANATE

GE:

Ghazz

Uighurs

XIXIA

JAPAN

NTINE EMPIRE

AR.

GHAZNAVID
EMIRATE
(Turkic)

TIBET

SONG
EMPIRE

FATIMID
CALIPHATE

BUWAYHID
EMIRATES

Arab nomads

minor Islamic
states

Burmese

NAN
CHAO

Taiwan

ANNAM

KURA

NEM

HADRAMAUT

**Hindu
kingdoms**

Pyu
state

Thais

Austronesians

CHAMPA

ALWA

YEMEN

Mon state

Chola state

KHMER
EMPIRE

Micronesians

Ceylon

minor Hindu and
Buddhist states

Celebes

*pastoral
nomads*

New Guinea

Borneo

*Papuan
farmers*

*eastern Bantu-speaking
herders and farmers*

Islamic
trading towns

Sumatra

SRIVIJAYA
EMPIRE

Melanesians

EAST JAVA

Java

Timor

Madagascar

Malagasy

*San hunter-
gatherers*

*Australian Aboriginal
hunter-gatherers*

c.900–1000

Polynesians

*Tasmanian
hunter-gatherers*

The World in 1279

By 1279, Western Europe was showing new confidence with the building of cathedrals, and crusades against the Muslims and Slavs. Islam had withstood these attacks from Christendom and expanded into India and west Africa, where the kingdom of Mali was a center of Muslim culture. In Asia, the nomadic Mongol peoples had expanded westward to create an empire that stretched from the Pacific Ocean to the Caspian Sea.

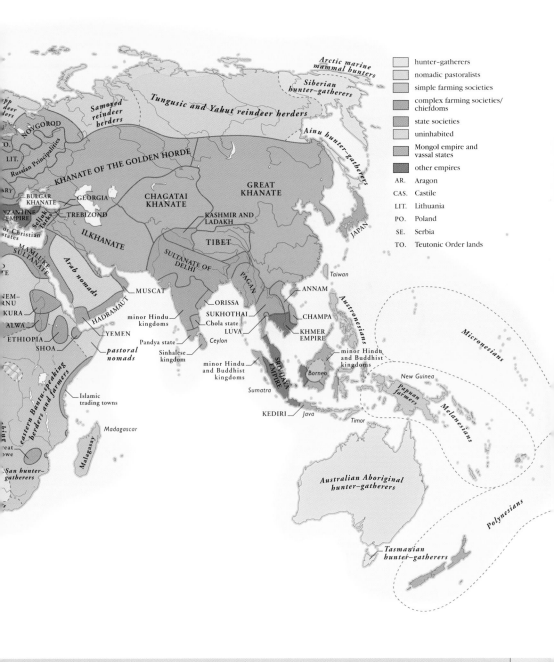

hunter-gatherers
nomadic pastoralists
simple farming societies
complex farming societies/
chiefdoms
state societies
uninhabited
Mongol empire and
vassal states
other empires

AR.   Aragon
CAS. Castile
LIT. Lithuania
PO.   Poland
SE.   Serbia
TO.   Teutonic Order lands

Arctic marine
mammal hunters

Siberian
hunter-gatherers

Tungusic and Yakut reindeer herders

Ainu hunter-gatherers

Samoyed
reindeer
herders

NOVGOROD

LIT.

Russian Principalities

KHANATE OF THE GOLDEN HORDE

CHAGATAI
KHANATE

GREAT
KHANATE

JAPAN

BULGAR
KHANATE

GEORGIA

YZANTINE
EMPIRE

TREBIZOND

Seljuk
Turks

ILKHANATE

KASHMIR AND
LADAKH

Christian
states

MAMLUKE
SULTANATE

Arab nomads

TIBET

SULTANATE OF
DELHI

Taiwan

NEM-
RNU

KURA

HADRAMAUT

PAGAN

ANNAM

Austronesians

ALWA

YEMEN

minor Hindu
kingdoms

ORISSA

SUKHOTHAI

CHAMPA

Micronesians

ETHIOPIA

SHOA

Chola state

LUVA

KHMER
EMPIRE

pastoral
nomads

Pandya state

Ceylon

Sinhalese
kingdom

minor Hindu
and Buddhist
kingdoms

eastern Bantu-speaking
herders and farmers

minor Hindu
and Buddhist
kingdoms

SRI-
VIJAYA
EMPIRE

Borneo

New Guinea

Papuan
farmers

Melanesians

Islamic
trading towns

Sumatra

Madagascar

KEDIRI

Java

Timor

Malagasay

San hunter-
gatherers

reat
we

Australian Aboriginal
hunter-gatherers

Polynesians

Tasmanian
hunter-gatherers

The World in 1492

By 1492, the Mongol empire had broken up and China had deliberately isolated itself from the rest of the world. On the borders of Europe and Asia, the Ottoman Turks ruled a large state around the Black Sea that stretched to the Balkans and threatened central Europe. To the north, Moscow had absorbed other Russian states and was expanding westward. In the Americas, the Inca and Aztec civilizations flourished.

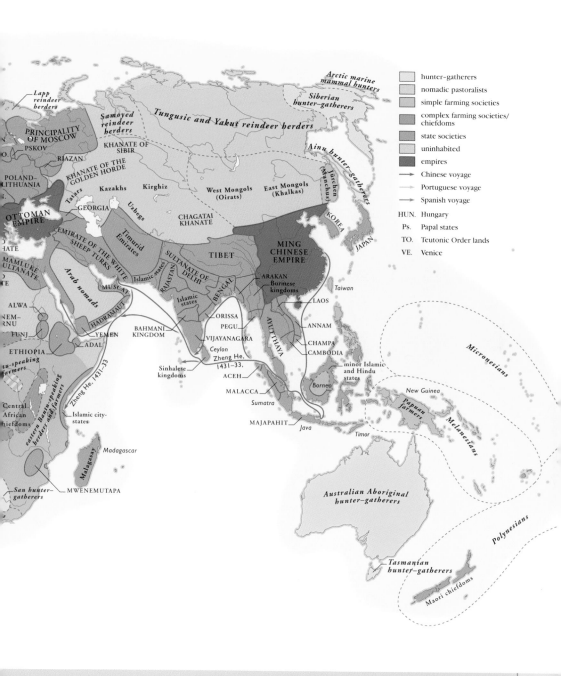

	hunter-gatherers
	nomadic pastoralists
	simple farming societies
	complex farming societies/chiefdoms
	state societies
	uninhabited
	empires
→	Chinese voyage
→	Portuguese voyage
→	Spanish voyage

HUN. Hungary
Ps.   Papal states
TO.   Teutonic Order lands
VE.   Venice

Lapp reindeer herders

Arctic marine mammal hunters

Siberian hunter-gatherers

Samoyed reindeer herders

Tungusic and Yakut reindeer herders

Ainu hunter-gatherers

PRINCIPALITY OF MOSCOW
PSKOV
RIAZAN
KHANATE OF SIBIR

KHANATE OF THE GOLDEN HORDE

POLAND–LITHUANIA

Kazakhs   Kirghiz   West Mongols (Oirats)   East Mongols (Khalkas)   Jürchen (Manchus)

OTTOMAN EMPIRE
...HATE
Tatars
GEORGIA
Uzbegs
CHAGATAI KHANATE

KOREA
JAPAN

EMIRATE OF THE WHITE SHEEP TURKS
Timurid Emirates
Islamic states
RAJASTAN
SULTANATE OF DELHI
TIBET
MING CHINESE EMPIRE

MAMLUKE SULTANATE

Arab nomads

MUSCAT
Islamic states
BENGAL
ARAKAN
Burmese kingdoms

Taiwan

ALWA
NEM-RNU
FUNJ
HADRAMAUT
YEMEN
ADAL

BAHMANI KINGDOM
ORISSA
PEGU
VIJAYANAGARA

LAOS
ANNAM
AYUTTHAYA
CHAMPA
CAMBODIA

Micronesians

ETHIOPIA
...tu-speaking farmers

Ceylon
Zheng He, 1431–33.
Sinhalese kingdoms
ACEH

minor Islamic and Hindu states

Borneo

MALACCA

New Guinea
Papuan farmers

Melanesians

Central African chiefdoms
eastern Bantu-speaking herders and farmers

Islamic city-states

Sumatra

MAJAPAHIT   Java

Timor

Zheng He, 1431–33

Madagascar
Malagasy

San hunter-gatherers
MWENEMUTAPA

Australian Aboriginal hunter-gatherers

Tasmanian hunter-gatherers

Polynesians

Maori chiefdoms

N

World Religions

Christianity, Islam, Hinduism, and Buddhism became established in Europe, Asia, and Africa in the period between 600 and 1500 CE.

ATLANTIC
OCEAN

Glasgow

Nidaras
(Trondheim)

Lincoln
York

SCANDINAVIA
Christianity, c.950–110

Salisbury
London
Canterbury

Uppsala

Rouen
Paris
Amiens
Cologne
Danzig

Roskilde

Santiago de
Compostela

Chartres
Bourges
Reims

Saxons
Christianity, 785

LITHUANIA
Christianity, 1386

León
Burgos

Strasbourg
Freiburg

Ulm

Prague
Christianity
c.1000

Poles

Russia
Christianity,

SPAIN
Christianity, 750–1492

Regensburg

Toledo
Seville
Córdoba

Milan

Vienna

Kiev

Fez
Tlemcen

Rome

Magyars
(Hungarians)
Christianity, c.1000

Bulgars
Christianity, 890

Constantinople

Mt Athos

BYZANTINE EMPIRE
Islam, 1071–1453

Bla
Se

TEKRUR
Islam, c.1030

Mediterranean Sea

Konya

GHANA
Islam, 1076

Niger

Timbuktu

MALI
Islam, c.1250

Masyaf

Bethlehem

Damascus
Jerusalem

Tanta
Cairo

Karba
Umm A

AIR
Islam, c.1350

Medina

Humaithira

Mecca

MAKKURA
Islam, 1317

Red Sea

ALWA

Axum

Lalibela

Debre Libanos

Harer

CONGO
Christianity, 1490

ETHIOPIA

Somal
Islam, c.1

Kilwa

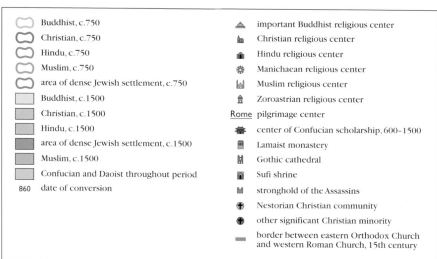

Buddhist, c.750
Christian, c.750
Hindu, c.750
Muslim, c.750
area of dense Jewish settlement, c.750
Buddhist, c.1500
Christian, c.1500
Hindu, c.1500
area of dense Jewish settlement, c.1500
Muslim, c.1500
Confucian and Daoist throughout period
860   date of conversion

▲ important Buddhist religious center
🏛 Christian religious center
🏛 Hindu religious center
✲ Manichaean religious center
Ⓜ Muslim religious center
🏛 Zoroastrian religious center
Rome   pilgrimage center
🏯 center of Confucian scholarship, 600–1500
🏛 Lamaist monastery
🏛 Gothic cathedral
🏠 Sufi shrine
Ⓜ stronghold of the Assassins
✚ Nestorian Christian community
✚ other significant Christian minority
━━ border between eastern Orthodox Church and western Roman Church, 15th century

World Religions

The birth of Islam, the most recent of the great world religions, originated in the teachings of the prophet Muhammad. It dominated the era known to Europeans as the Middle Ages, and it deeply affected all the established world religions.

Curriculum Context

Many curricula ask students to describe the life of Muhammad, the development of the early Muslim community, and the basic teachings and practices of Islam.

Martyrdom

Suffering death for one's religious faith.

From 610, Muhammad received a series of revelations which are recorded in the sacred book of Islam, the Koran. Islam drew much from Judaism and, to a lesser extent, Christianity; the Koran asserts that Muhammad is the last of a line of prophets that included Adam, Abraham, Noah, Moses, and Jesus.

Sunni and Shiite traditions

By the time of Muhammad's death in 632, Arabs had generally acknowledged him as their religious and political leader and had accepted Islam. The decades following his death were marked by disputes and civil war. From 680, the Shiite tradition of Islam developed, distinguished from the majority Sunni tradition by its stress on martyrdom and its radically different theories of religious leadership. In the ninth century, doctrinal disputes resulted in the secession from Shiism of the Ismaili sect. Until the 13th century, the Ismailis, or Assassins, murdered their enemies. The spread of both the Sunni and Shiite Islamic traditions was promoted by the growth, from the eighth century onward, of the mystical movement known as Sufism, which laid a heavy emphasis on piety and zeal.

Christianity

The rise of Islam halved the area under Christian domination between 600 and 750. Islam tolerated Christians, but the social and financial advantages of conversion were great, and Christianity soon declined in the areas conquered by the Arabs. Although Christianity regained some ground through missionary work and military conquest—most notably the

Crusades that temporarily restored Christian control to the Holy Land—it was again in retreat by the 15th century, as the Muslim Ottoman Turks overran the Byzantine empire and moved into the Balkans.

Hinduism

The Bakhti (devotional) revival movement in the 7th century allowed Hinduism to reassert itself against Buddhism, which had been dominant in the preceding centuries. The eighth-century philosopher Shankara gave impetus to the recovery by assimilating popular aspects of Buddhist devotion into Hinduism. A number of Hindus, especially from the lower castes, converted to Islam following the Muslim conquest around 1200, yet Hinduism remained India's principal religion.

Buddhism

Indian Buddhism, however, was destroyed by the Muslim conquest, continuing to flourish only in Sri Lanka. Buddhism also declined in Southeast Asia, following the introduction there of Islam in the 13th century. Chinese Buddhism reached the peak of its influence in the seventh and eighth centuries as a result of patronage by the Tang court. The period saw the spread of the meditative school of Chan (known in Japan as Zen) Buddhism and the populist Pure Land school which promised its adherents rebirth in paradise. Some 40,000 Buddhist temples and monasteries, all with tax-exempt estates, sprang up; they proved a severe drain on state income by 800. A brief imperial persecution in 845 closed many of these monasteries and forced 250,000 monks back into secular life. Buddhism recovered from this setback but never regained its former prestige.

The most important new converts to Buddhism in this period were the Tibetans. Elements of Tibetan shamanism were assimilated to Buddhism to form a distinctive tradition known as Lamaism.

Shamanism
A religion in which spirits of gods or ancestors are contacted by shamans, who are priests and diviners.

The Carolingian Empire

The most important event in western Europe between 600 and 800 CE was the founding of the Carolingian empire.

N

KINGDOM OF SCOTS
Iona
Dumbarton
STRATHCLYDE (Welsh)
Derry
Whithorn
Armagh
Kells
Lambay I
Bangor
St Davids

PICTISH KINGDOMS
Nechtan 685
Lindisfarne
NORTHUM
Jarrow
Whitby
York
MEI

IRISH KINGDOMS

WELSH PRINCIPALITIES
Cheddar
WESSEX
Portland

Tamworth
Ips
London
K
Hamwi

English Channel

Rouen
Neustria
Paris
Se

Landévennec
Rennes
Nantes
Noirmoutier

Bretons

Tours
Bourges
Poitiers 732

ATLANTIC OCEAN

Bordeaux

Basques
Oviedo
Covadonga 718
KINGDOM OF ASTURIAS
Galicia
Douro
Segoyuela 713

AQUITAIN
Moissac
Auch
Toulouse
Septimania
Roncesvalles 778

Zaragoza
Tortosa

Ger
Barcelona
Balearic Islands

UMAYYAD CALIPHATE
Tagus
Toledo
Lisbon
Guadiana

Córdoba
Seville
Ecija 711
Jerez de la Frontera 711
Algeciras

Alicante

UM

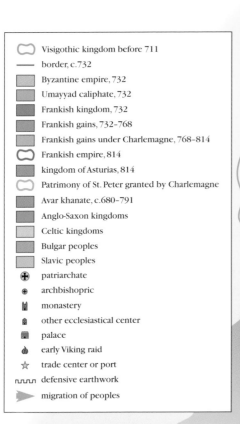

Visigothic kingdom before 711
border, c.732
Byzantine empire, 732
Umayyad caliphate, 732
Frankish kingdom, 732
Frankish gains, 732–768
Frankish gains under Charlemagne, 768–814
Frankish empire, 814
kingdom of Asturias, 814
Patrimony of St. Peter granted by Charlemagne
Avar khanate, c.680–791
Anglo-Saxon kingdoms
Celtic kingdoms
Bulgar peoples
Slavic peoples
⊕ patriarchate
⊕ archbishopric
🏰 monastery
🏛 other ecclesiastical center
▦ palace
💧 early Viking raid
☆ trade center or port
ᴖᴖᴖ defensive earthwork
➤ migration of peoples

Norse

Svear

Finns

L. Ladoga

☆ Staraja Ladoga

Kaupang ☆

Vänern

Birka ☆

Lake
Peipus

Slovianians

Vättern

Götar

Baltic Sea

☆ Grobin

Balts

Western Dvina

Mazovians

Danes

Ribe ☆

Hedeby ☆

Frisians

☆ Reric

Bardowick •

Abodrites

Pomeranians

Vistula

Poles

Magyars, c.800

×734

Scheessel •

Wiltzites

Derevlians

782 ×

Magdeburg ☆

• Dorestad

Saxons

• Paderborn

Elbe

Oder

mburg

Aachen

Cologne •

Sorbs

Volhynians

erstal

Prüm

Thuringia

Erfurt

Fulda

Metz •

Mainz

Frankfurt

Hallstadt

Thionville

Lorsch

Forchheim

Bohemians

St Emmeram

CARPATHIAN

Regensburg ☆

Goths

Alemannia

Lorch ☆

Danube

Besançon •

Salzburg ☆

St Gall

Bavaria

AVAR KHANATE

M T S

ALPS

Carinthia

Pannonia

rgundy

Aquileia ☆

Sava

BULGAR
KHANATE

ienne

Milan •

Pavia •

KINGDOM OF THE LOMBARDS

Venice ☆

Croats

Po

Black Sea

Bobbio •

Comacchio •

Serbs

Danube

Pliska ▣

Luna •

Ravenna •

Split •

Marseille

Exarchate
of Ravenna

DUCHY OF
SPOLETO

Vlachs

Ragusa •

Constantinople ✠

806,
807 ×

Corsica

• Spoleto

Farfa ▣

Dyrrhachium •

Thessalonica •

• Abydos

ANATOLIA

Rome ✠

Monte
Cassino

Benevento

Bari ☆

BYZANTINE EMPIRE
(Eastern Roman empire before 610)

Sardinia

Naples •

Salerno •

• Ephesus

Cagliari ✠

DUCHY OF
BENEVENTO

Athens •

Corinth •

O CALIPHATE

Palermo •

• Reggio

Sicily

Tunis •

Syracuse •

Rhodes

Cyprus

Malta

Mediterranean Sea

Crete

The Carolingian Empire

Of the Germanic kingdoms set up within the territory of the western Roman empire in the fifth century, only the Frankish and the Visigothic still survived in 600. The Visigothic kings preserved the late Roman administrative structure but they remained distant from their Hispano-Roman subjects. Faced with an invasion of Muslim Arabs and Berbers from North Africa in 711, the Visigoths received no support, and the kingdom abruptly collapsed.

Caliphate
The territory ruled by a caliph, who was the spiritual and earthly head of Islam.

The invaders overran most of the Iberian peninsula in only two years, bringing it within the Umayyad caliphate. Resistance was restricted to the mountains of the far north. Here the small Christian kingdom of Asturias developed, based at Oviedo. By 800, it had won back part of the northwest peninsula.

Frankish mayors
Since the mid-fifth century, the Merovingian dynasty had ruled the Frankish kingdom. They followed the Germanic custom of dividing the kingdom between all male heirs. The succession was rarely simple, and civil wars and assassinations were frequent. In the mid-seventh century, real authority passed into the hands of court officials known as the mayors of the palace. Frankish power declined, and some peripheral areas of the kingdom were lost for a time. Aquitaine, which broke away in 670, was not taken back until 768. The most successful of the mayors, Pepin II of Herstal, was ruler of the entire kingdom by 687. Founder of the Carolingian dynasty, he began an expansion of Frankish power. His son Charles Martel (mayor 714–41) turned back an Arab invasion at Poitiers in 732.

Papacy
The government of the Roman Catholic Church, headed by the pope.

Carolingian expansion
Charles' successor Pepin III (r.741–68) formed an alliance with the Papacy in 751. The year before, the Lombards (rulers of most of Italy since 568) had

conquered the Byzantine exarchate of Ravenna and were threatening Rome itself. In return for military aid, the pope authorized Pepin to assume the kingship of the Franks. Pepin died in 768, and the kingdom was divided between his two sons, Charlemagne and Carloman. On the latter's death in 771, Charlemagne was sole ruler; he doubled the size of the Frankish realm in 30 years of campaigning. He was also an energetic legislator and administrator. He promoted missionary activity among the pagan Saxons in the northeast and encouraged the revival of classical learning. Charlemagne made considerable donations of land to the Papacy and had himself crowned emperor by the pope on Christmas Day 800, an act he saw as restoring the Roman empire in the west.

Exarchate

A region ruled by an exarch, who was a Byzantine viceroy.

Curriculum Context

Carolingian success was built on the state's ability to maintain public order and local defense for the empire's subjects.

British kingdoms and Christianity

The Anglo-Saxons had overrun most of the fertile lowland zone of Britain by 600 and were beginning to form regional kingdoms, the most powerful was Northumbria, but it declined after defeat by the Picts in 685. In the eighth century, the Mercian kingdom rose to dominance under Aethelbald and Offa.

Western European trade revival

Frankish overrule brought a modest revival of trade and towns to western Europe, most marked around the southern North Sea and the Baltic, where ports and seasonal trading places developed by 800.

The Celtic Church

The Anglo-Saxon migrations into southern Britain had cut off British Christianity from contact with the Roman church. The Celtic church developed a distinctive identity and in Ireland it fostered the creation of a monastic civilization that was to have significant influence on cultural and religious life in Europe. Irish and Roman missionaries both won converts among the Anglo-Saxons in the seventh century. The Celtic church was persuaded to rejoin the Roman church in 664.

Viking Age Europe

The Vikings left their homelands in Scandinavia to establish new settlements across Europe between 793 and 1050.

Iceland
c.870 Norse settlement

c.986 to
Greenland

Faroe Islands
c.825 Norse
settlement

Shetland
Islands

Orkney
Islands

Hafrsfjord
885

Hebrides

KINGDOM
OF SCOTS

Iona
Scone

*North
Sea*

KINGDOM OF
STRATHCLYDE
(Welsh)

Lindisfarne

EARLDOM OF
NORTHUMBR

IRISH
KINGDOMS

KINGDOM
OF
YORK   York

Dublin

Ut

Limerick

KINGDOM
OF
WESSEX

DANELAW

Waterford   Wexford

WELSH
PRINCIPALITIES

Edington
878 London
Winchester

Dorest
EAS
(G

Dyle
891

Lorraine

Quentovic

Rouen

Normandy

Reims 955

Metz

914–39 occupied but
not settled by Vikings

Paris

926

Luxe

BRITTANY

Orléans

Loire

Nantes

Fontenoy
841

BURGUN

*ATLANTIC
OCEAN*

WEST
FRANCIA
(FRANCE)

Cluny

937

Lyon

PROVENCE

Bordeaux

951

NAVARRE

Oviedo

Toulouse

ARAGON

924

Arles

Marseille

Santiago de
Compostela

León

PYRENEES

Fraxi
890–9
pirate

KINGDOM OF
ASTURIAS AND
LEÓN

Douro

Zaragoza

Barcelona

951

Co

Tagus

Toledo

Sardir

Lisbon

Mérida

903

Guadiana

UMAYYAD EMIRATE

Balearic
Islands

Alicante

AC
E

Córdoba

Seville

IDRISID CALIPHATE

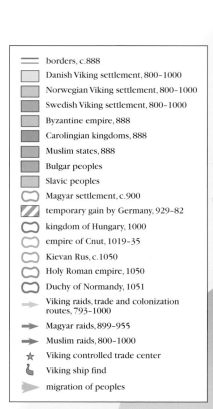

— borders, c.888

Danish Viking settlement, 800–1000

Norwegian Viking settlement, 800–1000

Swedish Viking settlement, 800–1000

Byzantine empire, 888

Carolingian kingdoms, 888

Muslim states, 888

Bulgar peoples

Slavic peoples

Magyar settlement, c.900

temporary gain by Germany, 929–82

kingdom of Hungary, 1000

empire of Cnut, 1019–35

Kievan Rus, c.1050

Holy Roman empire, 1050

Duchy of Normandy, 1051

Viking raids, trade and colonization
routes, 793–1000

Magyar raids, 899–955

Muslim raids, 800–1000

Viking controlled trade center

Viking ship find

migration of peoples

Trondheim

Svear
(Swedes)

WAY

Tune
Gokstad
Äskerkärr
Götar

ENMARK

kuldelev
Lund
Ladby   Roskilde

Abodrites
burg

Wolin

Pomeranians
Gniezno

Prus

Poles

Bohemians
Prague

Franconia
ensburg

Lechfeld
955
Bavaria
all

Aquileia
Venice

CROATIA
Patrimony
of St. Peter

Rome

DUCHY OF
BENEVENTO

Sicily

Malta

Finns

Lake
Onega

Finns

Lake
Ladoga

Beloozero

Staraja Ladoga

Sigtuna
Birka

Vänern

Vättern

Paviken
Gotland

Baltic Sea

Balts

Grobin

Kolobrzeg
Elbing

Vistula

Oder

Danube

Vienna

Slovaks

Gran
Pest

Pannonia
Moravians

Serbs

Belgrade

Otranto

Izborsk
Pskov

Lake
Peipus

Novgorod

KIEVAN RUS

Yaroslavl

Western Dvina

Gnezdovo

Viatchians

Chernigov

Kiev

Derevlians

Severyans

Dnieper

Magyars

Volga

Bulgar

Volga
Bulgars

KHAZAR KHANATE

Don

Volga

Sarkel

Itil

CARPATHIAN MTS

896–907

BULGAR
KHANATE

Pliska

Danube

Sava

Pechenegs

Goths

Tmutorokan

Black Sea

Constantinople
860

ANATOLIA

BYZANTINE   EMPIRE

Euphrates

Tigris

Cyprus

ABBASID
CALIPHATE

Mediterranean Sea

Crete

924

915

933

Riade

Elbe

921

921

927

846

827

Bari
840–71 Muslim
pirate base

Salzburg

Viking Age Europe

The Vikings—pagan raiders from Denmark and Norway—burst upon western Europe at the end of the eighth century as a bolt from the blue. The targets for their attacks were defenseless coastal monasteries that offered rich plunder. Their first known raid was against the monastery at Lindisfarne, Northumbria, in 793.

Curriculum Context

An important aspect of the Viking migrations and invasions is their effect on European countries, particularly on the emergence of independent lords and the knightly class.

In the 830s, the Vikings began to sail up rivers. In 865, a Danish army invaded England. Much of eastern and northern England was overrun and settled (the area known as the Danelaw, with its capital at York). The Wessex king Alfred (r.871–99) resisted the Danish advance. By 954, Alfred's successors had conquered the Scandinavians and created a united English kingdom.

Viking exploration and trade

The Vikings also established colonies in Normandy, Shetland, Orkney, Ireland, the Faroe Islands, and Iceland. A migration across the Atlantic about 1000 led to the colonization of Greenland and the first European exploration in the Americas. In eastern Europe, Swedish venturers known as Rus pioneered trade routes along the rivers of Russia to the Black and Caspian Seas, giving their name to the Russian state that developed at Novgorod around 862.

Scandinavian society

By the late eighth century in Scandinavia, power was becoming centralized, creating an intensely competitive society. Viking pirate raids overseas became a means to acquire wealth and an armed following to support their ambitions at home. Other Vikings sought to conquer lands abroad.

Viking and Slav states

During the 10th century, Denmark and Norway emerged as stable territorial states, followed by

Sweden by the 12th century. In this period began the Scandinavians' conversion to Christianity. Denmark's hegemony briefly included England and Norway under Cnut (r.1016– 35). In the east, the Slavs assimilated the Rus ruling class. By 1000, Kievan Rus was a powerful Slavic state, influenced by the Byzantines who introduced Orthodox Christianity. In Normandy, the Vikings adopted French culture and language by 1000, but remained independent of the French monarchy.

Hegemony
Influence or authority over others.

End of the Carolingian empire

The Viking invasions occurred while the Carolingian empire which had dominated Europe was weakened by internal squabbles. The emperor Louis the Pious (r.814–40) refused to divide the empire equally between his sons. Louis' younger sons and many of the Franks regarded the settlement as unjust and in 827, civil war broke out. The Treaty of Verdun (843) saw the empire divided into three parts. By this time, royal authority was weakened and defenses against the Vikings had collapsed. The Carolingian empire finally broke up in 889 into five kingdoms: West Francia (France), East Francia (Germany), Italy, Burgundy, and Provence.

Muslim and Magyar raiders
Muslim pirates from Spain and Tunisia raided the Mediterranean coast and preyed on travelers over the Alpine passes. In the east, a nomadic people, the Magyars, crossed the Carpathians around 900 to settle in the Danube plain, from where they raided Italy, Germany, and France. By 1000, however, the Muslim and Magyar threats had ended.

The beginnings of the Holy Roman Empire
Carolingian rule in Germany ended in 911, and power passed to the Saxon kings. Otto I (r.936–73) defeated the Magyars at Lechfeld (955), and they converted to Christianity. Otto annexed the kingdom of Italy in 951–61. Crowned Roman emperor in 962, he founded what became known as the Holy Roman empire.

Annexed
Incorporated within another state.

Feudal Europe

Feudalism was the dominant political system in western Europe between 1050 and 1300.

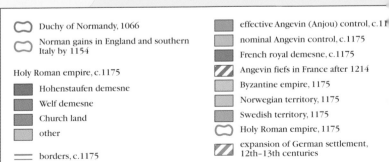

	Duchy of Normandy, 1066		effective Angevin (Anjou) control, c.11
	Norman gains in England and southern Italy by 1154		nominal Angevin control, c.1175
			French royal demesne, c.1175
	Holy Roman empire, c.1175		Angevin fiefs in France after 1214
	Hohenstaufen demesne		Byzantine empire, 1175
	Welf demesne		Norwegian territory, 1175
	Church land		Swedish territory, 1175
	other		Holy Roman empire, 1175
	borders, c.1175		expansion of German settlement, 12th–13th centuries

Finns

Lake Onega

ndheim

Y

SWEDEN

Uppsala

Åbo

Vänern

Vättern

Visby

Lund

MARK

Baltic Sea

Revel

Estonians

Lake Peipus

Livs

Riga

Western Dvina

Danzig

Königsberg

Wends

Stettin

Brandenburg

Prus

Vistula

POLAND

Breslau

Krakow

Prague

BOHEMIA

Vienna

Salzburg

Austria

Styria

Gran

thia

leia

Venice

VENICE

na

ace

Zara

Ragusa

Benevento 1266

Naples

Bari

KINGDOM OF SICILY

Palermo

Sicily

Malta

Beloozero

River Neva 1240

Ladoga

Lake Ladoga

REPUBLIC OF NOVGOROD

Novgorod

Lake Peipus 1242

Pskov

PRINCIPALITY OF VLADIMIR

Volga

Bulgar

Volga Bulgars

Lithuanians

Polotsk

PRINCIPALITY OF POLOTSK

Minsk

PRINCIPALITY OF TUROV-PINSK

Pinsk

PRINCIPALITY OF VOLHYNIA

Galich

PRINCIPALITY OF GALICIA

Moscow

Vladimir

Murom

PRINCIPALITY OF SMOLENSK

Smolensk

PRINCIPALITY OF CHERNIGOV

Chernigov

PRINCIPALITY OF KIEV

Kiev

PRINCIPALITY OF PEREYASLAV

Pereyaslav

Ryazan

PRINCIPALITY OF MUROM-RIAZAN

PRINCIPALITY OF NOVGOROD-SEVERSK

Don

Dnieper

Cumans (Turkic)

to Kiev

to Kiev

Cumans (Turkic)

Volga

Alans

Pest

HUNGARY

Sava

Belgrade

Danube

Black Sea

GEORGIA

BYZANTINE EMPIRE

Dyrrachium

Thessalonica

Constantinople

Mediterranean Sea

Crete

Lombard league city, 1167

German city founded in 13th century

ION fief of the Papacy during the pontificate of Innocent III, 1198–1216

German and Danish crusades against the p Slavs and Balts, 12th–13th centuries

Swedish expansion, 12th–13th centuries

western limit of Mongol conquests, 1240

Spanish states, 1300

Aragon

Castile

emirate of Granada

Portugal

controlled by the Teutonic Knights, c.1300

Russian states

pagan area

Feudal Europe

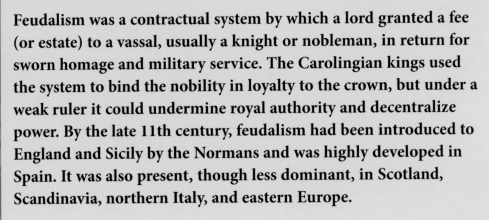

Feudalism was a contractual system by which a lord granted a fee (or estate) to a vassal, usually a knight or nobleman, in return for sworn homage and military service. The Carolingian kings used the system to bind the nobility in loyalty to the crown, but under a weak ruler it could undermine royal authority and decentralize power. By the late 11th century, feudalism had been introduced to England and Sicily by the Normans and was highly developed in Spain. It was also present, though less dominant, in Scotland, Scandinavia, northern Italy, and eastern Europe.

Vassal

A person who swears to obey a lord in return for protection.

Curriculum Context

The way in which monarchies expanded their power at the expense of feudal lords is important in understanding the growth of centralized monarchies in Europe.

By 1200, the military importance of feudalism was in decline, as kings could raise money to hire professional soldiers, vassals could make a cash payment in lieu of military service, and fees had become heritable.

French royal lands and fees

Decentralization was most extreme in France, where the royal lands (the demesne) were confined in the 11th century to the area around Paris and Orléans, while powerful vassals like the dukes of Normandy and the counts of Anjou and Aquitaine were semi-independent rulers of vast fees. When William of Normandy became king of England by conquest in 1066, he became more powerful than his feudal lord, the French king. In the 1150s, Henry Plantagenet of Anjou accumulated fees covering half of France. In 1154, he inherited the English throne to become, as Henry II, the most powerful ruler in Europe. Philip Augustus (r.1180–1223) revived the French monarchy and recovered all the Angevin fees except Gascony. In 1214, he repulsed a German invasion at Bouvines, making France the strongest power in Europe.

German kings and the church

The German kings and emperors granted land as fees to the church. Literate priests and abbots administered its fees. Celibate churchmen could not found dynasties, so the lands returned into the gift of the king. As long as the king retained control over appointments, this system countered the territorial nobility. When emperor Henry III died in 1056, leaving his son Henry IV (r.1056–1106) in the control of a weak regency, the Papacy asserted itself. The ensuing dispute over the right to nominate to vacant sees, gave the popes greater authority. A sign of their new prestige was the calling of the First Crusade in 1095.

Fall of the Hohenstaufen dynasty

The Hohenstaufen emperor Frederick Barbarossa (r.1152–90) found his authority challenged in Germany by powerful territorial princes. He tried to tighten imperial control in Italy but was defeated by the Lombard league of cities in 1176. Although the Hohenstaufens won control of Sicily in 1194, they failed to assert their authority over the German princes, and the Holy Roman empire disintegrated into a loose federation of states. The emperor Frederick II (r.1210–50) was faced with the hostility of the papacy and the Lombard cities, and his reign ended in failure. The Hohenstaufen dynasty was overthrown in 1266. Despite the political fragmentation of the empire, the 13th century saw German influence expand to the east through the establishment of peasant settlements and new towns, and the activities of traders and the crusading order of the Teutonic Knights in the Baltic.

Slavic states and Mongol invasions

The Slavic state of Kievan Rus broke up into several principalities in 1132, most of which were overrun by the Mongols in 1237–41. Alexander Nevsky (r.1236–63), ruler of Novgorod, submitted voluntarily to the Mongol invasion and was therefore able to concentrate his resources on resisting incursions by Swedish forces and the Teutonic Knights. In 1252, he added the principality of Vladimir to his possessions.

Regency
Government by a person or persons while a sovereign is too young or disabled to govern, or in the absence of the sovereign.

See
The region containing a cathedral, over which a bishop has power.

War, Revolt, and Plague

In the 14th century, Europe suffered religious disagreements, many wars, and the Black Death epidemic that killed one-third of its population.

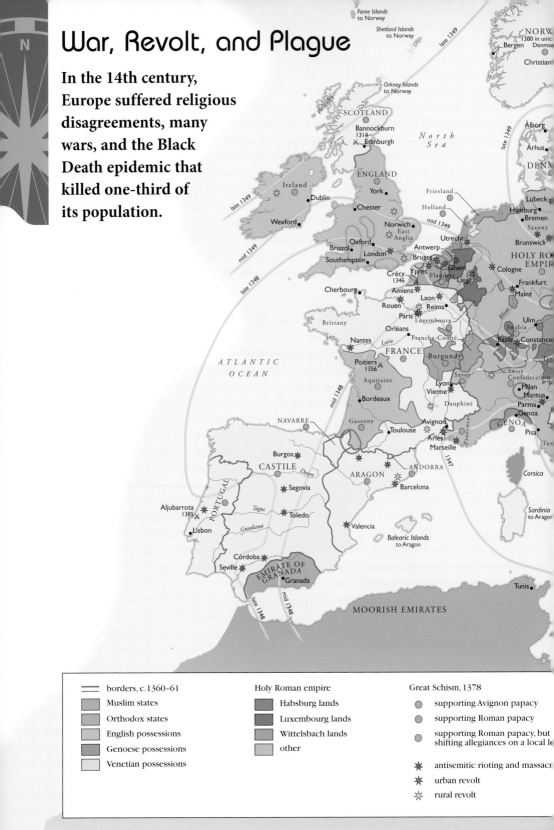

borders, c.1360–61

Muslim states

Orthodox states

English possessions

Genoese possessions

Venetian possessions

Holy Roman empire

Habsburg lands

Luxembourg lands

Wittelsbach lands

other

Great Schism, 1378

supporting Avignon papacy

supporting Roman papacy

supporting Roman papacy, but shifting allegiances on a local le

antisemitic rioting and massacr

urban revolt

rural revolt

SWEDEN
1397 in union with
Denmark

Åbo

Revel

Stockholm

Vättern

Visby
1361

Gotland
to Denmark

Calmar

gen

Baltic Sea

Riga

Königsberg

Danzig

Teutonic Knights

Vistula

Warsaw

POLAND

Silesia

Oder

Krakow

Bohemia

Vienna

Austria

mid 1349

Buda

Pest

Styria

HUNGARY

Sava

Belgrade

Zara

BOSNIA

RAGUSA

PLES

Durazzo

Thessalonica

Messina

LY

Malta
to Sicily

Mediterranean

Lake
Ladoga

REPUBLIC OF
NOVGOROD

ROSTOV

Novgorod

Lake
Peipus

PSKOV

western Lithuania

Vilna

LITHUANIA

1350

Kiev

Dnieper

RUTHENIA

Lemberg

MOLDAVIA

mid 1348

late 1349

late 1348

WALLACHIA

Danube

Nish

Nicopolis
1396

BULGARIAN STATES
1393 Ottoman vassals

Kosovo
1389

SERB STATES
1397 Ottoman vassals

Constantinople

BYZANTINE EMPIRE

Gallipoli

1347

TVER

Moscow

MUSCOVY

Kulikovo
1380

SMOLENSK

VLADIMIR-SUZDAL

MUROM

1351

RYAZAN

KHANATE OF THE
GOLDEN HORDE

1351

mid 1348

1347

1346

Sarai

Volga

Kaffa

1346

Black Sea

1347

Trebizond

GEORGIA

Ankara

OTTOMAN
SULTANATE

Smyrna

TURKISH EMIRATES

Tigris

LESSER
ARMENIA

Euphrates

1347

DUCHY OF
ACHAEA

to Byzantine
empire

to Sicily

KNIGHTS OF
ST JOHN

Rhodes

Crete

CYPRUS

Cyprus

Famagusta

JALAYRID
SULTANATE

1347

Sea

1347

1347

Alexandria

Cairo

MAMLUKE SULTANATE

lands acquired for Burgundy by
Philip the Bold, c.1396

spread of Black Death, with date

area relatively lightly affected
by the Plague

Lollard heretic movement, c.1400

War, Revolt, and Plague

The authority of the Papacy—already in decline in the face of royal attempts to build centralized nation-states—faced a further setback in 1303, when it fell under the domination of the French monarchy. In 1309, the Papacy took up residence at Avignon. It returned to Rome in 1377, but a disputed papal election led to the Great Schism in 1378, with rival popes in Rome and Avignon. The schism was unresolved until 1417 and divided Europe.

France supported the Avignon Papacy, so England—then involved in the Hundred Years' War (1337–1453) with France—supported the Roman Papacy, while Scotland, England's enemy, joined the French party.

War in France

The Hundred Years' War was sparked off by French attempts to recover English lands in France. After English victories at Crécy (1346) and Poitiers (1356), the French ceded Aquitaine and Gascony, but when a 28-year truce was agreed in 1396, the English held less French land than they had in 1337. In 1363, the French monarchy granted the duchy of Burgundy to Philip the Bold, the younger son of John II. Through marriage, Philip later gained the wool towns of Flanders and the imperial county of Burgundy (the Franche-Comté).

War in central and eastern Europe

War was endemic throughout the Holy Roman empire. The powerful city-states of northern Italy engaged armies of mercenaries to fight one another. The German princes were occupied in dynastic struggles to control imperial elections. From 1377–89, the princes formed a united front to reduce the independence of the cities of south Germany and the Rhineland. In 1388, after a century of rebellion, the Swiss confederation of eight cantons secured their independence from the dukes of Habsburg. In eastern Europe in 1354, the

Curriculum Context

Students studying the Hundred Years' War should focus on its causes and consequences.

Canton

A small territorial division of a country.

Ottoman Turks took Gallipoli on the European shore of the Dardanelles; by the end of the century, they had overrun most of the Balkans. Political conflicts and the paralysis of the Papacy ensured that there was no purposeful response to the Ottoman threat.

The Black Death arrives in Europe

The Black Death, a combined epidemic of bubonic and pneumonic plague, broke out on the east Asian steppes in the 1330s and spread along the Silk Road to reach the Genoese port of Kaffa in the Crimea in late 1346. From here it was carried (by the parasitic fleas that infested ships' rats) to Venice, Genoa, and Marseille and then spread quickly along the main trade routes of Europe. A series of crop failures earlier in the century had caused extensive famines in overpopulated areas, and the effects of malnutrition probably weakened resistence to the disease. Even in the most lightly affected areas, 10 to 15 percent of the population died, and in the worst affected areas (Tuscany, East Anglia, and Norway), mortality may have been 50 percent or more. Around a third of Europe's population died between 1346 and 1351, and the plague remained endemic in Europe for 250 years.

Effects of the Black Death

Outbreaks of the plague were often accompanied by religious hysteria. Jews and foreigners were blamed and attacked. Depopulation caused prices and rents to fall and wages to rise, loosening the traditional bonds of service. Uprisings such as the Jacquerie wars in northern France (1358) and the English Peasants' Revolt of 1381 were frequent. Mob violence was mainly directed at landlords, tax officials, and rich urban oligarchies. There was often an element of anticlericalism, found also in the rise of heretical movements such as the Lollards in England. In eastern Europe, the peasantry had serfdom imposed upon them by lords who were anxious not to lose tenants.

Curriculum Context

Many curricula ask students to analyze major changes in the agrarian and commercial economies of Europe in the context of drastic population decline.

Oligarchy

A government controlled by a small group of people.

Economy of Medieval Europe

The period between 1000 and 1500 was a time of agricultural improvements, urbanization, increased production of goods, and the establishment of important trading associations and centers.

falcons, sulfur, walrus ivory
from Greenland and Iceland

Faroe Islands to Norway

Tro

Shetland Islands to Norway

Christiania timber

Bergen

Stavanger

Orkney Islands to Norway

fish

SCOTLAND

North Sea

Alborg

Viborg

butter

Copenhagen

DENMARK

Edinburgh

copper coal

Kiel

Wi

Lübeck

Hamburg

wool

Dublin

wool

York

Hull

fish

Bremen

salt

lead, copper

Chester

Lincoln

Boston

Groningen

wool

Kampen

Deventer

Brunswick

Ma

Stourbridge

King's Lynn

Norwich

Yarmouth

Ipswich

linen

Osnabrück

copper

ENGLAND

wool

Bristol

London

Damme

Utrecht

Nijmegen

Dortmund

pottery

iron

Southampton

Plymouth

tin

St Omer

Bruges

Ypres

Ghent

Antwerp

silk

Louvain

Cologne

HOLY ROMA

EMPIRE i

Lille

Liège

Brussels

Frankfurt

Rouen

Arras

Douai

Tournai

Mainz

Worms

lead

Nuren

St Denis

Reims

Metz

salt

Guibray

Paris

Provins

Bar-sur-Aube

Nördlingen

Strasbourg

Augsbu

Brest

linen

Lagny

Orléans

Tours

Troyes

Besançon

Zurzach

linen

sa

linen

FRANCE

silk

Dijon

Geneva

Innsb

Nantes

salt

Poitiers

Brescia

La Rochelle

Milan

silk

ATLANTIC OCEAN

Lyon

silk

Pavia

Piacenza

Parma

Mant

Bordeaux

to England

Genoa

Modena

Bolog

silk

Lucca

Fo

La Coruña

iron

Bayonne

Toulouse

Albi

silk

Beaucaire

Pisa

Florer

iron

NAVARRE

iron

Montpellier

Arles

salt

Marseille

Siena

Orvieto

iron

st

León

Villalón

ANDORRA

iron

Perpignan

to Mallorca

Corsica to Genoa

salt

Viterbo

Rome

Oporto

Valladolid

wool

Zaragoza

Barcelona

Colmbra

Salamanca

CASTILE

ARAGON

Tortosa

Balearic Islands

Sardinia to Aragon

silver

salt

Sicily

Lisbon

Toledo

silk

Valencia

Palma

PORTUGAL

olive oil

Badajoz

Guadiana

salt

hides

MALLORCA

Córdoba

silk

Seville

silver

GRANADA

Murcia

Jerez

Málaga

Granada

Almería

Cádiz

EMIRATE OF GRANADA

Tangiers

hides

Melilla

gold

Algiers

gold
from central and southern Africa

Annaba

Tunis

MOORISH EMIRATES

gold
from central and southern Africa

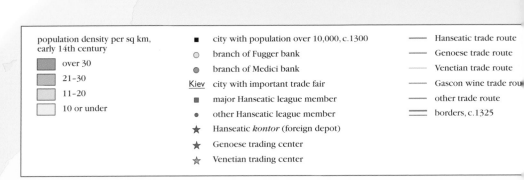

population density per sq km, early 14th century

- over 30
- 21–30
- 11–20
- 10 or under

■ city with population over 10,000, c.1300
◦ branch of Fugger bank
◉ branch of Medici bank
Kiev city with important trade fair
■ major Hanseatic league member
• other Hanseatic league member
★ Hanseatic *kontor* (foreign depot)
★ Genoese trading center
☆ Venetian trading center

—— Hanseatic trade route
—— Genoese trade route
—— Venetian trade route
—— Gascon wine trade rou
—— other trade route
══ borders, c.1325

Economy of Medieval Europe

Over 90 percent of the population of medieval Europe were peasant farmers. The manorial system—by which a lord divided up an estate (the manor) among individual peasants who farmed it—was widespread. The lord was expected to protect his peasants in times of war, provide relief in times of famine, and administer justice, in return for payments of produce, labor, and money.

Curriculum Context

In some states, students are asked to understand how technology impacts social development. Agriculture in medieval Europe is a good example.

Many peasants were unfree serfs, tied for life to the land on which they worked and passing their unfree status onto their descendants. By the end of the Middle Ages, serfs had been replaced by tenant farmers and wage laborers in the British Isles, Italy, and Iberia.

Agricultural improvements

Around the year 700, a three-field system of crop rotation was widely adopted: one field was used for cereals, one for vegetables such as beans, and the third left fallow, to preserve soil fertility. The introduction of the wheeled plow and of the padded shoulder collar that enabled horses to be used for plowing, allowed the heavy soils of northern Europe to be worked more efficiently. Productivity was boosted, and peasant prosperity increased. Most surplus produce was sold at local markets, but wool, hides, wine, dairy products, salt, fish, and grain were traded in large quantities over long distances. Moving goods by land was slow, so most bulk trade went by sea or river. Mining, ore smelting, logging, charcoal burning, quarrying, and salt extraction were also important.

Urban trade and industry

Except in Italy, urban life declined dramatically in western Europe during the late Roman empire. Italy remained the most urbanized region of Europe throughout the Middle Ages. Medieval European towns were small and rarely had populations above 10,000.

They were unhygienic places and, as deaths exceeded births, they relied on immigration from the countryside to maintain their populations. Citizenship, and with it a right to participate in local government, was normally restricted to property owners. The trade and craft activities of towns were regulated by associations of merchants or craftsmen known as guilds. These prescribed standards of quality and training and excluded outside competition. Production of high-quality goods for export was important in some areas, such as Flanders, where there was a flourishing woolen textile industry. Seasonal trade fairs were important commercial events, attracting merchants from a wide area; some developed into major centers of international business.

Baltic and Mediterranean trade

One of the most powerful trade associations of the Middle Ages was the Hanseatic League, membership of which extended to 37 north German and Baltic towns at its peak in the 14th century. It negotiated trading privileges for its members, prepared navigational charts, suppressed piracy, and even waged war. It maintained offices and depots in many cities. The league's power declined at the end of the Middle Ages, when it was faced with greater competition from England and the Netherlands. In the Mediterranean, maritime trade was dominated by the cities of Venice and Genoa. Both took advantage of the Crusades to build up trade links with Asia, the source of luxury products such as silks, spices, and gems.

Capitalism and finance

By the 13th century, merchants were financing craft production, so that productivity increased, but craftsmen lost their independence. International banking houses such as the Medici and the Fuggers emerged, and the principles of modern insurance and accountancy were established.

Renaissance Europe

The Renaissance was a cultural movement in 15th-century Europe, a period in which political boundaries were constantly changing.

SHETLAND
1469 to Scotland

Bergen•

ORKNEY
1468 to
Scotland

Loth... of the Isles

SCOTLAND

1460–88
recovered by
Scotland

Edinburgh•

ENGLAND
Towton
1461 ×
York

Bre

Haarlem
Amsterda
Devent
1477
Utrecht
1472

Chester
Bosworth Field
1485 ×
Norwich

Irish Pale
•Dublin
Shrewsbury
1403
Wales
Oxford
1478
London
1476

Irish

Bristol•

Southampton•
Bruges
Calais•
Ghent
Antwerp
1470
Brussels
1474

Cola
1466

Frank

Agincourt
1415
PICARDY
Rouen
×Formigny
Paris
1470
Reims
Luxembourg

×
Nancy
1477
Base
14
1462

St
14

BRITTANY
Normandy
1429

Nantes•

Tours
Orleans
Loire
Bourges•
Burgundy
FRANCE

Dijon
Cluny
1483
Franche-
Comté s
Con

Geneva
1478

ATLANTIC
OCEAN

Castillon
1453
Bordeaux•×
Gascony

Lyon
1473
Savoy
14

Mil

Geno

NAVARRE

Avignon
Provence

León•
Burgos
1490
Douro
ANDORRA

Corsica

Barcelona
1475
ARAGON

Madrid•

Tagus

CASTILE
1479 union of crowns
with Aragon

Valencia
1475

Balearic
Islands
to Aragon

Sardinia

Lisbon
1489

PORTUGAL

Guadiana

GRANADA
1485–92
to Castile

Seville
1492

Cádiz•
Málaga
Granada•
Almería•
Cartagena•

Tangier
1471
Asilah
1471
Ceuta
1415

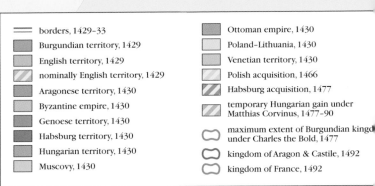

═══ borders, 1429–33	▨ Ottoman empire, 1430
▨ Burgundian territory, 1429	▨ Poland-Lithuania, 1430
▨ English territory, 1429	▨ Venetian territory, 1430
▨ nominally English territory, 1429	▨ Polish acquisition, 1466
▨ Aragonese territory, 1430	▨ Habsburg acquisition, 1477
▨ Byzantine empire, 1430	▨ temporary Hungarian gain under Matthias Corvinus, 1477-90
▨ Genoese territory, 1430	◠ maximum extent of Burgundian kingd under Charles the Bold, 1477
▨ Habsburg territory, 1430	
▨ Hungarian territory, 1430	◠ kingdom of Aragon & Castile, 1492
▨ Muscovy, 1430	◠ kingdom of France, 1492

KINGDOM OF DENMARK
(Union of Calmar)

Åbo

Lake
Ladoga

MUSCOVY

Sweden

Stockholm
1483

Helsinki

Revel

PRINCIPALITY OF
NOVGOROD
1478 to Muscovy

Novgorod

1463–74
to Muscovy

Yaroslavl

Rostov

Kazan

Vänern

Vättern

Lake
Peipus

Pskov

Tver
1483 to Muscovy

1408, 1447, 1451, 1465, 1472, 1480

Calmar

mark

Copenhagen
1493

Lübeck
mburg

Stettin

Danzig

Riga

Königsberg

Vilna

Smolensk

Moscow

Ryazan

Sarai

RYAZAN

KHANATE OF THE
GOLDEN HORDE
Tatars

Western Dvina

Tannenberg
1411

TEUTONIC KNIGHTS

Brandenburg
Berlin

eipzig
1481

Breslau

Krakow

POLAND–LITHUANIA

Warsaw

Vistula

Lemberg

Odra

OMAN
RE
mberg
0
Nuremberg
470

Prague
1478

Bohemia

Dnieper

Augsburg
1468
Munich
1482
Innsbruck

Salzburg

Vienna
1482

Austria

Buda

Danube

Pest

HUNGARY

MOLDAVIA

Kaffa
1475 to Ottomans

Venice
1469

Zagreb

Sava

Belgrade

WALLACHIA

Black Sea

GEORGIA

ntua

Rimini
Urbino

VENICE

Zara

Split

Serbia

Danube

Nish

1444

Varna

Florence
1471
PAPAL
STATES
Rome
1467

Subiaco
1465

RAGUSA

Bosnia

Montenegro

Sofia

Adrianople

Trebizond

TREBIZOND

NAPLES
1442 to Aragon

OTTOMAN

Constantinople
1488
1453 to Ottomans

TURKISH
EMIRATES

BENEVENTO

Naples

ALBANIA

Otranto

EMPIRE

Ankara
1402

Palermo

Reggio
1480

ATHENS

Eubœa

Sicily

Morea

KNIGHTS OF
ST JOHN

Rhodes

Malta

CYPRUS
1489 to Venice

Cyprus

MAMLUKE
SULTANATE

Mediterranean
Sea

Crete

Muscovy, 1492

Ottoman empire, 1492

Portuguese base

printing center, with date

Milan early Renaissance cultural center

Tatar campaign

Hussite movement, 1415–36

Renaissance Europe

The Renaissance, the great cultural movement of 15th-century Europe, had its origins in the revival of interest in classical philosophy, science, and literature that first emerged during the 12th century. Its immediate roots lay in 14th-century Italy in the work of artists and humanist scholars. By the early 15th century, new styles of painting and sculpture were evolving, and classical forms of architecture were being revived.

Aristocracy

A small, privileged minority with great influence in government.

Curriculum Context

Students can demonstrate and explain the influence of ideas by analyzing the social and intellectual significance of the technological innovation of printing with movable type.

In the 15th century, Italy's city-states came to be ruled by dynastic princes. Italian Renaissance rulers dispensed patronage to secure prestige and influence. In Venice, an urban aristocracy was keen to publicize its wealth and status. Printing, developed in Germany in the mid-1450s, aided the spread of the new arts and learning outside Italy. By the early 16th century, these were finding their place in the courts of Europe's new monarchs, who were emerging from periods of rivalry and civil war with strong centralized governments.

French and English wars

In the early 15th century, France was divided by the rivalry between the Burgundian and Armagnac families. Henry V of England (r.1413–22) seized the opportunity to reopen the Hundred Years' War. His major victory at Agincourt (1415) and conquest of northern France led to his recognition as Charles VI's heir in 1420. After Henry's death, English fortunes declined. By 1453, England had lost all of France except Calais. Defeat provoked the dynastic Wars of the Roses in England, until Henry VII (r.1485–1509), founder of the Tudor dynasty, restored stable government.

Burgundy and the Habsburgs

The dukes of Burgundy profited from France's troubles to enhance their own position by forming an alliance with the English which lasted until 1435. Under Philip the Good (r.1419–67), they acquired further territory in the Netherlands. His successor, Charles the Bold, wanted to establish an independent kingdom and tried to build a corridor of lands to link his southern and northern possessions but died in battle against the Swiss in 1477. When his heiress Mary married Maximilian of Habsburg, the Burgundian lands passed to the Habsburgs, rulers of the Holy Roman empire since 1438. Louis XI (r.1461–83) seized and retained the lands of the duchy of Burgundy in France.

Iberian conquest and exploration

In the Iberian peninsula, a century or more of rivalry between Castile and Aragon (which added the kingdom of Naples to its extensive Mediterranean empire in 1442), came to an end in 1469 with the marriage of Ferdinand of Aragon to Isabella of Castile. Under their joint leadership, Granada, the last Muslim state in Spain, was conquered in 1485–92. Portugal, prevented from expanding in the peninsula by Castile, turned its attention to North Africa, beginning with the capture of Ceuta in 1415. In the 1430s, Portuguese navigators began to explore the African coast and in 1487, entered the Indian Ocean. Even more significant was the voyage of Columbus, commissioned by Isabella of Castile, which led to the "European discovery" of the New World in 1492.

Eastern European states

Eastern Europe saw the creation of a strong but short-lived kingdom: Poland–Lithuania, under Casimir IV (r.1447–92) the largest state in Europe. Hungary, which resisted Ottoman expansion in the Balkans, dominated central Europe under Matthias Corvinus (r.1477–90). By 1500, Muscovy had absorbed most of the other Russian principalities. With the fall of the Byzantine empire in 1453, it was left as the only significant Orthodox state. Ivan III married a Byzantine princess in 1472, adopting the title of *czar* (caesar).

Duchy
The territory ruled by a duke.

Curriculum Context

The resurgence of centralized monarchies and economically powerful city-states in western Europe in the 15th century was closely associated with the cultural flowering of the Renaissance.

Arab Conquests

The rise of Islam led to Arab political unity, conversion to Islam, and conquests in Western Asia, North Africa, and Iberia between 632 and 750 CE.

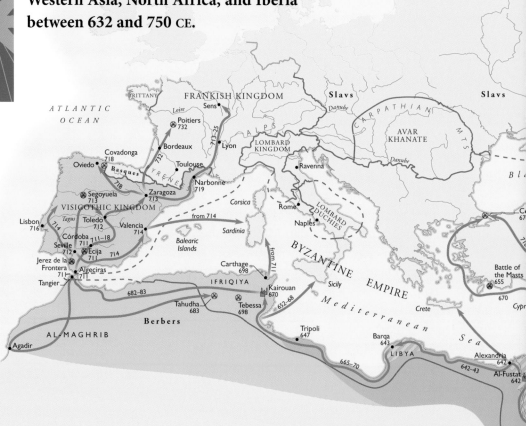

border at the death of Muhammad, 632

Arabs practicing Islam, 632

growth of the Arab caliphate

at the death of Abu Bakr, 634

at the death of Uthman, 656

at the fall of the Umayyad dynasty, 750

Monophysite Christians within the Byzantine empire

Arab campaign or raid, with date

Amsar (Arab military settlement), 638–670

Umayyad mosque

Umayyad palace

Kufa Umayyad cultural center

Arab victory

Arab defeat

battle between Arabs

Azd Arab tribe

expansion of Chinese Tang empire

Bulgars

Khazars

Alans

CAUCASUS MTS

751

Caspian Sea

Aral Sea

WESTERN TURK
KHANATE

713

FERGHANA

early 8th century

Amu Dar'ya

ARMENIA

Ardebil
643

TABARISTAN

Bukhara
710

Samarkand
710

SOGHD

Balkh
652

HINDU KUSH

Indus

KASHMIR

Edessa
639

Harran

MESOPOTAMIA

Aleppo
638

Hamah
635

Qazvin
643

637-43

Rayy
643

ZAGROS

Jafula
638

Tigris

Euphrates

Nehavend
642

SASANIAN

KHORASAN

Merv
650

Herat
650

652

652

Kabul
664

Multan
713

Yamuna

Tripoli
638

Karbala
680

Ctesiphon
637

Wasit

PERSIA

EMPIRE

SEISTAN

Helmand

EMPIRE OF
HARSHA

Damascus
635

Quseir Amra

Qasr el Mshatta

Kufa
638

Al Qadisiya
637

633-38

MTS

Persepolis
648

650

Mu'tah
629

Ghassan

Kalb

Lakhm

Basra
638

Bakr

643

SIND

Indus

Gurjaras

633-38

640

633-38

BAHRAYN

Siraf

MAKRAN

Valabhi

Persian Gulf

637-43

Ghatafan

HEJAZ

Juhcina

Mt Uhud
625

Medina

632-33

Kinda

Hanifah

Al-Yamama
632

OMAN

Red Sea

Bedr
624

Sulaym

Quraysh

Mecca

Hawazin

ARABIA

Battle of
the Camel
657

633-38

Mahrah

632-33

AXUM

Azd

HADRAMAUT

YEMEN

Himyar

Arab Conquests

The great empires of the Mediterranean and West Asia had for centuries been accustomed to raids by Arab border tribes. Though troublesome, these raids were prevented from becoming a serious threat by the political disunity of the Arabs. However, this situation changed dramatically in the early seventh century as a result of the rise of Islam.

Monotheism
The belief that there is only one god.

Theocratic
Governed by people who are guided by a god or by divine beings.

The faith of Islam (meaning "submission to the will of God") was founded by Muhammad (c.570– 632), a member of the Meccan Quraysh tribe. Muhammad's espousal of monotheism met with opposition from the Quraysh, so to escape persecution, the prophet and his followers fled in 622 to Medina. Muhammad used Medina as a base to fight the Quraysh and in 630, he returned to Mecca in triumph. However, Muhammad continued to live at Medina, which became the capital of a theocratic Islamic state, and used diplomacy and force to spread Islam to other Arab tribes.

Conquest and division

Muhammad was succeeded by his father-in-law Abu Bakr, the first caliph (successor). After putting down an anti-Islamic rebellion, Abu Bakr completed the political and religious unification of the Arabs. Under the next two caliphs, Umar and Uthman, the Arabs began an explosive expansion, conquering the rich and populous Byzantine provinces of Syria, Palestine, Egypt, and Libya and completely destroying the Persian Sasanian empire. On Uthman's death, civil war broke out between supporters of the caliph Ali, Muhammad's son-in-law, and Muawiya, a member of Uthman's Umayyad family. After Ali's murder in 661, Muawiya became caliph, founding the Umayyad dynasty. Islam split into its two main branches: the Sunnites (from *sunna*, "tradition of Muhammad"), who formed a majority, and the Shiites (from *shi'atu Ali*, "party of Ali").

The Umayyad period

Arab expansion continued under the early Umayyads. By 715, the Islamic caliphate, extending from the Indus and central Asia to the Pyrenees, was the largest state the world had yet seen. Yet its attempts to complete the conquest of the Byzantine empire and the west failed, with unsuccessful sieges of Constantinople in 677 and 717 and defeat by the Franks in 732.

Umayyad achievements

The Umayyads introduced hereditary succession, claiming divine appointment and demanding total obedience. By adapting Byzantine bureaucracy, they created an administrative system capable of ruling a world empire. As this empire could not be ruled effectively from the remote Arabian city of Medina, Muawiya moved the capital to Damascus in 661. The Umayyad period saw the beginning of Arabization of the conquered populations through conversion to Islam, the adoption of Arabic as a common language, and intermarriage. During the Umayyad period, the first mosques were constructed as centers for Islamic worship.

Unified Arabs, divided enemies

Many factors explain the swift rise of the Arabs in the seventh century. Before Islam, intertribal feuding had played a major role as a means of winning status and booty. Muhammad's unification of the Arabs channeled the warrior tradition into raids on the neighboring Byzantine and Sasanian empires. The united Arab armies, now larger and more effective, rapidly overran new territories. The Sasanian empire was riven by civil war after its defeat by Byzantium, and organized resistance quickly collapsed after the Arab victory at Nehavend in 642. The Byzantine empire also had internal problems. The Monophysite Christian populations of Syria, Palestine, and Egypt, who had suffered years of persecution by Constantinople, welcomed the Arabs as liberators. Similarly, the Visigothic kingdom of Spain also collapsed through internal divisions.

Curriculum Context

Important aspects of Arab conquest in the seventh century are their defeats of the Byzantines in Syria and Egypt, and the Sasanids in Persia and Iraq.

The Arab World Divided

From 750 to 1037, religious conflicts and tribal feuding divided the Arab world.

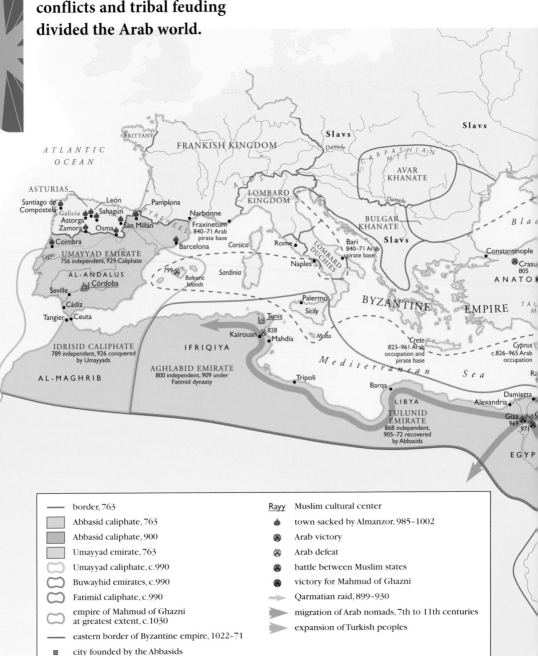

ATLANTIC OCEAN

FRANKISH KINGDOM

BRITTANY

Slavs

Danube

CARPATHIAN MTS

AVAR KHANATE

Slavs

ASTURIAS

Santiago de Compostela
Galicia
León
Astorga
Zamora
Osma
Sahagún
San Millán
Coimbra

Pamplona

PYRENEES

Narbonne
Fraxinetum 840–71 Arab pirate base
Barcelona

LOMBARD KINGDOM

ALPS

Danube

BULGAR KHANATE

Bla

UMAYYAD EMIRATE
756 independent, 929 Caliphate

Tagus

AL-ANDALUS
Córdoba

Seville

Cádiz

Tangier
Ceuta

IDRISID CALIPHATE
789 independent, 926 conquered by Umayyads

AL-MAGHRIB

799

Balearic Islands

Corsica

Sardinia

Rome

LOMBARD DUCHIES

Naples

Palermo

Sicily

Tunis

Kairouan
828
Mahdia

IFRIQIYA

AGHLABID EMIRATE
800 independent, 909 under Fatimid dynasty

Tripoli

Malta

Bari 840–71 Arab pirate base

Slavs

Constantinople

BYZANTINE EMPIRE

Crasu 805

ANATO

TAL
M

Crete 823–961 Arab occupation and pirate base

Cyprus c.826–965 Arab occupation

Mediterranean Sea

Ra

Barqa

LIBYA

TULUNID EMIRATE
868 independent, 905–72 recovered by Abbasids

Damietta
Alexandria

Giza 969
971

EGYP

——— border, 763	
▦ Abbasid caliphate, 763	
▦ Abbasid caliphate, 900	
▦ Umayyad emirate, 763	
⌒ Umayyad caliphate, c.990	
⌒ Buwayhid emirates, c.990	
⌒ Fatimid caliphate, c.990	
⌒ empire of Mahmud of Ghazni at greatest extent, c.1030	
——— eastern border of Byzantine empire, 1022–71	
■ city founded by the Abbasids	
🕌 Abbasid mosque	
⛪ Abbasid palace	
🕌 Umayyad mosque	
⛪ Umayyad palace	

Rayy Muslim cultural center
♠ town sacked by Almanzor, 985–1002
⊗ Arab victory
⊗ Arab defeat
⊗ battle between Muslim states
⊗ victory for Mahmud of Ghazni
➤ Qarmatian raid, 899–930
➤ migration of Arab nomads, 7th to 11th centuries
➤ expansion of Turkish peoples

Volga Bulgars

Turks

Pechenegs, 10th century

Khazars

CAUCASUS MTS

Caspian Sea

Aral Sea

River Talas ⊗
751

Seljuks (Ghuzz), 1028–38

Qarakhanids 990–99

CHINESE TANG EMPIRE

SAMANID EMIRATE
874 independent

TIBET

GEORGIA
788 independent

Trebizond

KHWARIZM

SOGHD

•Samarkand

•Bukhara

Amu Darya

Indus

ARMENIA
886 independent

mon

•Edessa
•Harran
Mosul ⊗⊗ Battle of
the Zab
750

Dabiq

Raqqa

JAZIRA

SYRIA

AZERBAIJAN

Qazvin•

Tigris

ZAGROS

DAYLAM

⊗ Rayy
811

Merv ⊗
999

⊗ Balkh
1007

KHORASAN

Nishapur•

Kabul•

Peshawar
1009

HINDU KUSH

•Ghazni

Helmand

Thaneswar•

KASHMIR

Ganges

Qasr al Hayr
(2 palaces)

•Damascus

Jabal Says

Samarra•

Hamadan•
Nehavend•

⊗ Baghdad
813

•Wasit

Kufa•

IRAQ

Basra•

Isfahan

PERSIA

Kerman•

•Istakhr

Shiraz•

Siraf•

SEISTAN

Arabs of Multan
871 independent

•Multan

Arabs of Sind
871 independent

Indus

MAKRAN

Multan•

Delhi•

Gurjara–Pratiharas

erusalem

SAFFARID EMIRATE
903 independent, 908 annexed by the
Samanid emirate

HEJAZ

Persian Gulf

Qarmatians

•Muscat

OMAN
903 independent

Medina•

•Mecca

Red Sea

ARABIA
899 independent

RA

AXUM

ZAYDITE EMIRATE
860 independent

•San'a

The Arab World Divided

The authority of the Umayyad caliphs was undermined in the eighth century by Shiite–Sunni conflict, tribal feuding among the Arabs, and discontent among new converts to Islam in the conquered lands. Rebellion broke out in the province of Khorasan, and Abu al-Abbas of the Sunni Abbasid family was proclaimed caliph by the rebels. Following an Abbasid victory in 750, there was a massacre of the Umayyad family.

Emirate

A state ruled by an Islamic chief known as an emir.

One of the few to survive, Abd al-Rahman (r.756–88), escaped to Spain and seized power in Córdoba in 756. His founding of an independent emirate began the political fragmentation of the Arab world. Abd al-Rahman faced internal opposition for several years, which allowed the Christians of Asturias to regain Galicia. The Franks were also able to recapture Narbonne. The Abbasid caliphate suffered further losses in 789, when the Idrisid emirs of the Maghrib founded a Shiite caliphate. In 800, the Aghlabid emirs of Ifriqiya (Tunisia) also became independent.

A golden age of Islamic civilization

The Abbasid caliphate's vast wealth, acquired partly from the exploitation of rich silver mines in the Hindu Kush Mountains, funded lavish building projects and patronage of the arts and sciences. Baghdad, founded as a new capital to replace Damascus in 763, had within 40 years become probably the world's largest city and its greatest cultural center. The assimilation of Persian literature and Greek science and philosophy to Islamic and Arab tradition initiated a period of great achievements in many intellectual fields. Medieval Europe would owe most of its knowledge of medicine, astronomy, geography, and mathematics to Arab scholars. Strict observance of Islam did not preclude tolerance of the faith of people of other religions, while Arabs were no longer accorded a privileged status.

Curriculum Context

Curricula may ask students to evaluate Abbasid contributions to mathematics, science, medicine, and literature.

Decline and fall of the Abbasids

The Abbasids reached their zenith under Harun al-Rashid (r.786–803), but civil war broke out between his sons after his death. The caliph's authority began to decline in favour of the provincial emirs. In 868, Egypt and Palestine became independent under the Tulunids, while the eastern provinces seceded under the native Persian Saffarid and Samanid dynasties. The Abbasids lost Arabia after the rebellion of the Shiite Qarmatian sect in 899. The Christians of Armenia had also regained their independence in 886. In 914, the Fatimids, who had come to power in Ifriqiya in 909, began the conquest of Egypt; by 1000, they were the dominant Islamic power. In about 913, the Shiite Buwayhids, a tribal confederation from Daylam, conquered Persia. Their capture of Baghdad in 945 ended Abbasid territorial power.

Secede
To withdraw from a state or an organization.

Mahmud and the Ghaznavid emirate

The rise of the Buwayhids was accompanied by the decline of the Samanid emirate. Its northern provinces were lost to the Qarakhanid Turks in the 990s, while the rest was seized by a rebel Turkish mercenary, Mahmud of Ghazni. Thereafter, Mahmud expanded into the Buwayhid emirates and northern India. He conducted holy wars against the Hindu kingdoms, destroying Hindu temples. The Ghaznavid emirate was the first of the Turkish empires of West Asia, yet it declined rapidly following an invasion by the Ghuzz Turks led by members of the Seljuk clan in 1037.

Curriculum Context

Describing the diverse factors that influenced the ability of the Muslim government to rule an empire that stretched from western Europe to India and China helps students understand cause-and-effect relationships.

The Umayyad emirate in Spain

After its initial setbacks, the Umayyad emirate in Spain consolidated its position and in 929, Abd al-Rahman III (r.912–61) declared himself caliph. He conquered the Maghrib in 973, and his general Almanzor (al-Mansur) had victories over the Christians of the north. However in 1008, civil war broke out, the caliphate collapsed, and Muslim power in Spain never fully recovered.

The Byzantine Empire

The Byzantine empire was a continuation of the eastern Roman empire that existed in southeastern Europe and Turkey between the 7th and 13th centuries.

LOMBARD KINGDOM

640

751

Venice c.1000

Ravenna

Exarchate of Ravenna

Sirmium

Sirmium

Belgrade

KH

Genoa

Zara

Split

Serbs

Nish

Corsica

Dalmatia

Ragusa

Rome

LOMBARD DUCHIES

Bulgaria

Dyrrachium 1081

Th

Gaeta 1063

Naples 1130

Bari

Amalfi 1127

Longibardia

Otranto

Sardinia

Nicopo

Nicopo

Cephalonia

Calabria

Palermo

Reggio

Taormina

Catania

Sicily

Carthage

827

Pantano Longarini

Malta

AFRICA

669-70

LIB

Legend

border, 628	
Byzantine empire, 628	
Byzantine empire, 867	
Byzantine empire, 1025	
border of Byzantine themes, 1025	
Byzantine empire, 1204	
semi-autonomous Byzantine enclave, with date of loss	
Bulgar khanate, 986	
Norman kingdom of Sicily, c.1090	

- ⊗ Byzantine victory
- ⊗ Byzantine defeat
- Byzantine shipwreck
- major fortified city
- fortress
- Mistra major Byzantine cultural center
- → military campaigns
- ⇒ Arab expansion

Dnieper

Bulgars 679

Rus (Vikings) 860, 907, 941

Dniester

Dorostalon
971

Danube

Nicopolis

Pliska

Paristrion

Mesembria
817

Philippopolis

Adrianople

Arcadiopolis
970

1204

670–77, 716–17

Constantinople

Bosporus

Cherson

Cherson

Black Sea

Sinope

Amastris

Paphlagonia

Armeniakon

Trebizond

Chaldia

Ani

Theodosiopolis

ARMENIA

ista

Strymon

Philippi

Macedonia

Thrace

Nicomedia

Optimaton

Nicaea

Bucellarion

Gangra

Ancyra

Amasia

Colonea

Colonea

Theodosiopolis

Seljuk Turks, 1071–80

Vaspurakan

Manzikert
1071

Mt Athos

Pelagos

Abydos

Opsikion

Mytilene

Dorylaeum

Amorion

Charsianon

Sebastea

Anatolia

Caesarea

Sebastea

Mesopotamia

Meletine

Iberia

Taron

Aghtamar

Chios

Smyrna

Sardes

Myriocephalum
1176

Cappadocia

Arabissos

Melitene

Lycandos

Samosata
873

Edessa

Poleis

Parephratidiai

SASANIAN EMPIRE
642 conquered by Arabs

Thebes

Athens

Aegean

Samos

Ephesus

Laodicea

Thracesion

Anatolikon

Iconium

Tyana

Loulon

Cilicia

Tarsus

Teleuch

Tigris

Attalia

Yassi Ada

Cibyrrhaeoton

Serçe
Liman

Rhodes

Myra

Rhodes

Seleucia

Seleucia

Antioch

Antiochia

Aleppo

SYRIA

Euphrates

633–40

637–43

Crete

Gortyn

Crete

Cyprus

Cyprus

Mediterranean Sea

Tyre

Caesarea

Damascus

Yarmuk River
635

633–40

633–40

PALESTINE

Jerusalem

Alexandria

642–43

Heliopolis
640

EGYPT

Nile

640

Arabs

The Byzantine Empire

The Byzantine empire is the term used to describe the continuation of the eastern Roman empire after the accession of Heraclius (r.610–41). When he came to the throne, the empire was facing defeat by the Persian Sasanian empire. Heraclius reformed the army and administration to create a new state. Greek, which had always been the majority language of the eastern Roman empire, replaced Latin as the official language of government.

Heraclius' reforms saw Byzantium emerge victorious from its war with Persia in 627. However, the exhausted empire was unprepared for attacks by the Arabs, newly united by Islam, that began in 633.

Curriculum Context

Students studying the Byzantine empire should be able to explain how the Byzantine state withstood Arab Muslim attacks between the 7th and 10th centuries.

Byzantine territorial losses

Syria, Palestine, Egypt, and North Africa were lost by 698, but Arab attempts to take Constantinople in 670–77 and 716–17 failed. The Lombards captured Genoa in 640 and the exarchate of Ravenna in 751. The Bulgars overran much of the Balkans in 679. The Arabs began the conquest of Sicily in 827.

The Macedonian dynasty

The shrinkage of the empire was reversed by the emperors of the Macedonian dynasty (867–1059), who restored the frontiers in the north and the east close to where they were in late Roman times. Under Basil II (r.976–1025; the "Bulgar-slayer"), the Byzantine empire reigned supreme in southeast Europe and West Asia.

Military recruitment

The resilience of the empire was chiefly a result of the system of *themes*, or military recruitment districts, introduced by Heraclius. In return for tax and military service, soldiers were settled as free peasants on land in the *themes*, whose civil governors also acted as army commanders in wartime. This system produced well-motivated local forces that could be called up swiftly and which gave the state a reliable source of revenue. Originally numbering 13, the themes had grown to over 40 by the 11th century. After Basil II's death, the system was neglected by weak rulers who feared the army, so the empire was unprepared for invasion.

Curriculum Context

Comparing Byzantium's imperial political system with that of the Abbasid state helps students understand differing values and institutions.

The fall of Byzantium

Within 20 years of Basil II's death, the empire was again losing ground. By 1071, the Normans had largely driven the Byzantines out of Italy. In the same year, a crushing defeat by the Seljuk Turks at Manzikert was followed by the loss of Anatolia, the empire's main source of army recruits. The loss of Anatolia was a fatal blow for the empire. Although the western districts were regained by Alexius I Comnenus (r.1081–1118), the *themes* had been obliterated, and the area depopulated. The empire was left dependent on expensive mercenaries. The state was further impoverished in the 12th century as Venice and Genoa took control of Byzantine trade. Byzantium's prestige and diplomacy maintained the semblance of a great power, until the Seljuks inflicted another crushing defeat, at Myriocephalum, in 1176. The Fourth Crusade's capture and plunder of Constantinople delivered the fatal blow in 1204. Although the Byzantines retook their capital in 1261, the empire was a shadow of its former self.

Byzantine cultural influence

For most of the Middle Ages, Byzantium was Christendom's most sophisticated state, producing outstanding sacred art, literature, and architecture. Yet its frequent schisms with the western (Roman) church engendered mutual suspicion and hostility. As a result, Byzantium's cultural influence was strongest in areas where Orthodox Christianity prevailed: the Balkans, Georgia, and, especially, Russia.

Medieval Turkish Empires

Turkish states were established in Central and West Asia from the 11th century onward, and the Ottoman state became especially powerful in the 14th century.

Moldavia

Belgrade
1456

Bosnia

CRIMEA

Khanate of Crimea

Serbia

Kaffa

Wallachia

Kosovo
1389

Nicopolis
1396

Varna
1444

Black Sea

Bulgaria

Edirne
(Adrianople)
1361

Thrace

Constantinople
1453

Sinope

Thessalonica

Gallipoli

Nicaea

Eskisehir
(Dorylaeum)
1289

Trebizond

Bursa
1326

Ankara
1402

Köse Dagh
1243

Söğüt
1265

1097

DANISHMEND
EMIRATE

Sulaiman Ibn Qutlumish, 1080

SELJUK SULTANATE OF RUM

Myriocephalum
1176

ANATOLIA

Iconium

Aegean Sea

TAURUS MTS

LESSER
ARMENIA

Crete

Rhodes

Edessa
1086

Harran

Antioch

Aleppo
1258-61

Al-Qadmus
Khawabi
Tripoli

Masyaf

SYRIA

Cyprus

Syrian
Desert

PALESTINE

Damascus

Mediterranean Sea

LIBYA

'Ain Jalut
1260

Damietta

Gaza

Jerusalem
1099

1098

Alexandria

Cairo

Egypt

Aqaba

Medina

Mecca

Nile

Red Sea

Seljuk sultanate at maximum extent, 1092 (upon death of Malik Shah)

border, 1095

Byzantine empire, 1095

Seljuk territory lost to Byzantines and Crusaders, 1097–99

Fatimid caliphate, 1095

Zangid emirate under Nur al-Din, c.1174 (Ayyubid emirate from 1177)

Khwarizm shahdom, c.1220

Ottoman Turks under Osman I, c.1300

Ottoman empire, c.1360

Ottoman empire including vassal states, c.1492

Seljuk campaigns, with date

Mongol invasions, with date

route of Ottoman advance into Europe

Turk victory

Turk defeat

Ottoman capital, with date

Assassin stronghold

Turk nomads   Karakhanids

1219

Aral Sea

Jend
1219

Otrar

1219

Tashkent

1221

1028–38

Urgench

KHWARIZM

Bukhara

1220

Samarkand

1221

Caspian Sea

Derbent

azars

SOGHD

Amu Dar'ya

1258–61

Dandangan
1040

Baku

Jurjen

Merv

Balkh

Indus

1221

HINDU KUSH

Parvan
1221

Kabul

Peshawar

armenia

Araks

Nishapur
1038

1220

1221

Afghanistan

Sialkot

Chenab

Lake rmia

Tabriz

Berzem
1072

KHORASAN

1258–61

Ghazni

Punjab

Alamut

1220

1258–61

1258–61

Herat

Helmand

1042

Rayy
1220

Toghril Beg, 1040–42

1258–61

Multan

Sutlej

Kermanshah

Hamadan

GREAT SELJUK
SULTANATE

Dasht-e Lut

SEISTAN

GHAZNAVID EMIRATE

1055

ZAGROS MOUNTAINS

Isfahan

1229–31

PERSIA

Kerman

Baghdad

Indus

Basra

Shiraz

Persian Gulf

Siraf

Gulf of Oman

Arab nomads

ARABIA

Muscat

Oman

Medieval Turkish Empires

Turkish power in West Asia grew rapidly after the Seljuk invasion of the Ghaznavid emirate in 1037. Three years later, under Toghril Beg (r.1038–63), they had occupied the emirate's western provinces. In 1054–55, the Seljuks, heeding an appeal for help by the Abbasid caliph of Baghdad, drove the Buwayhids from the city. As Sunni Muslims, the Seljuks accorded the caliph greater respect than had the Shiite Buwayhids.

Under Toghril Beg's successor, Alp Arslan (r.1063–72), the Seljuks overran Syria and routed the Byzantines at Manzikert. In the reign of his successor Malik Shah (r.1072–92), Byzantine Anatolia was occupied, and the Fatimids expelled from Palestine.

Fragmentation of the Seljuk sultanate

Malik Shah's death sparked civil war, and the Seljuk sultanate began to fragment. By 1100, there were dozens of independent Seljuk states. The Byzantine empire and the First Crusade deprived the Seljuks of western Anatolia and northern Syria.

Syria and Egypt

Turkish power in the west recovered under Zangi, the governor of Mosul (r.1127–46), who united northern Syria and recaptured Edessa from the Crusaders. Zangi's son Nur al-Din (r.1146–74) conquered the rest of Muslim Syria and destroyed the Shiite Fatimid caliphate of Egypt. Saladin, Kurdish governor of Egypt, rebelled against the Zangids and, by 1177, controlled the emirate. The Ayyubid dynasty founded by Saladin held power until 1250, when the Mamlukes, a caste of mainly Turkish slave soldiers, seized power.

Caste
A social class with its own occupations and restrictions.

Mongol invasions

In the east, Turkish power continued to wane in the 12th century. Then in the early 13th century, the eastern Seljuk states were absorbed by a new Turkish power, the shahdom of Khwarizm. However, its growth was abruptly halted by the Mongol invasion of 1219. At a stroke, Chingis Khan broke the shahdom's power. The Seljuks of Rum were reduced to vassals in 1243, the Abbasid caliphate was destroyed in 1258, and in 1260, the Mongols drove the Mamlukes out of Syria. Although the Mamlukes recovered much of this territory later that year, the Mongols remained the dominant power in West Asia until Timur the Lame's death in 1405.

Rise of the Ottomans

Following the Mongol conquests, the Seljuk sultanate of Rum broke up. The Byzantine empire was now too weak to benefit, while the Serbs, Bulgars, and Latins were busy arguing over its dying remains. The Ottoman state began its growth under the minor Anatolian chief Osman I and by the death of Orhan (r.1324–60), the Ottomans occupied most of northwest Anatolia and had begun to expand into Europe, capturing Gallipoli in 1354. In 1361, Murad I (r.1360–89) captured Adrianople and, renaming it Edirne, transferred the capital there. Timur the Lame's invasion in 1402, and his victory at Ankara, led to the temporary collapse of the sultanate, but the Ottomans rallied quickly, expanding again by 1430. Constantinople, and with it the Byzantine empire, fell in 1453. Further expansion into central Europe was checked by the Hungarians at Belgrade in 1456.

A major factor in Ottoman success was the weakness of the neighboring Christian and Turkish states. The divisions in Europe caused by the Hundred Years' War and the Great Schism precluded a concerted Christian resistance. The Seljuks were weakened by the Mongols. Religious zeal was another vital element. Commitment to spreading the faith through holy war motivated the Ottoman armies.

Shahdom

A territory ruled by a shah in Greater Iran (an area including modern Iran, Turkmenistan, and Uzbekistan, and parts of Afghanistan, Kazakhstan, Tajikistan, and Kyrgyzstan).

Curriculum Context

Many curricula ask students to analyze the origins and early expansion of the Ottoman state up to the capture of Constantinople in 1453.

The Crusades

The Crusades were religious wars that took place from 1096 to 1291 between the Christian world and its Muslim enemies.

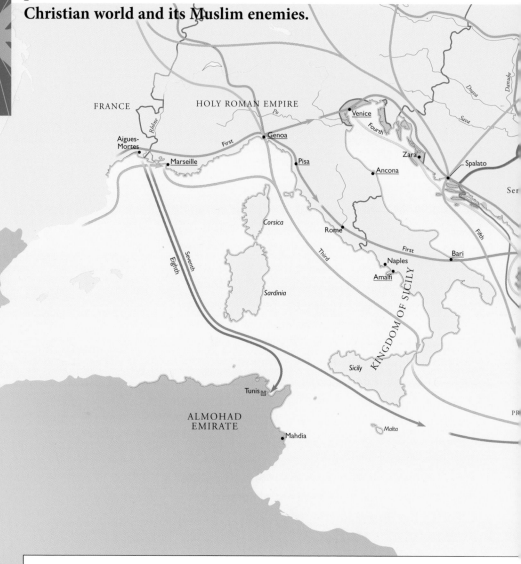

FRANCE

Aigues-Mortes
Marseille
Rhône

HOLY ROMAN EMPIRE

Po
Genoa
First
Pisa
Venice
Fourth
Zara
Ancona
Spalato
Drava
Sava
Danube
Ser

Corsica
Rome
First
Bari
Fifth
Third
Naples
Amalfi
Seventh
Eighth
Sardinia

KINGDOM OF SICILY

Sicily

Tunis

ALMOHAD EMIRATE

Mahdia
Malta

PR

—— border, c.1144	**Crusades**	⊗ Crusader victory
◯ Byzantine empire, c.1144	→ First, 1096–99	⊗ Crusader defeat
Byzantine states, 1204	→ Third, 1190–91	⛫ castle of the Military Orders
Islamic states, 1204	→ Fourth, 1202–04	⛫ other Crusader castle or fortified town
Venetian territory, 1204	→ Fifth (main army), 1217–21	⛫ Muslim castle or fortified town
Crusader territory, 1204	→ Seventh, 1248–54	⛫ Assassin castle
Crusader territory lost by 1204	→ Eighth, 1270	<u>Pisa</u> city with important trade links to the Holy Land, c.1200

The Crusades

The Crusades were holy wars fought to defend the Catholic church and the Christian people against those who were regarded as external and internal enemies of Christendom. Although the main crusading effort was directed against the Muslims in the Holy Land, Crusades were also conducted against the pagan Slavs of the Baltic, Muslim Spain, the Ottoman Turks in the Balkans, and heretics, such as the Cathars, within western Christendom itself.

The main period of crusading activity lasted from 1096 to 1291. It saw eight major campaigns and dozens of smaller expeditions.

The First Crusade

Curriculum Context

Many curricula ask students to analyze the causes and consequences of the European Crusades against Syria and Palestine.

The First Crusade was called by Pope Urban II in 1095 to help the Byzantine emperor Alexius I Comnenus against the Seljuk Turks. The main army, mostly French and Norman knights, fought its way across Anatolia to Antioch and on to Jerusalem, which was taken in 1099. Four Crusader states were set up in Syria and Palestine: the Kingdom of Jerusalem, the County of Tripoli, the Principality of Antioch, and the County of Edessa.

The Second and Third Crusades

Muslim unity began to be restored by Zangi, governor of Mosul, who retook Edessa in 1144; this loss prompted the Second Crusade (1147–49), which achieved nothing. The loss of Jerusalem after Saladin's victory at Hattin in 1187 led to the Third Crusade under Richard I (Lionheart) of England and Philip II Augustus of France. This failed to recover Jerusalem but did ensure the survival of the Crusader states.

Later Crusades

In the 13th century, it became clear that Christian control of the Holy Land could never be secure so long as Egypt remained the center of Muslim power. The

Fourth Crusade (1202–04) was called with the intention of attacking Egypt, but it never reached its destination. Assembled in Venice, the Crusaders were unable to pay for their transit to Egypt, and so agreed to help the Venetians capture the Hungarian city of Zara. Thereafter, the Crusade was diverted to Constantinople to back a claimant for the Byzantine throne who promised support for the expedition. When this support was not forthcoming, the Crusaders sacked Constantinople and made it the center of a Latin Empire.

Claimant
Someone who asserts a right to a title or territory.

Armed pilgrimages

The Crusaders saw their role as part of the pilgrimage tradition. Pilgrimages to holy places were undertaken as penance and to acquire spiritual merit. The ultimate pilgrimage was to Jerusalem, and when the Turks began to harass pilgrims in the 11th century, an armed pilgrimage to restore Christian control was thought fully justified. As an inducement, the papacy offered Crusaders spiritual and legal privileges, most important of which was remission of the penances due for sin. This was popularly interpreted as a guarantee of immediate entry to heaven if the Crusader were to die on the expedition.

The Fifth Crusade (1217–21) was defeated by river flooding as it advanced on Cairo. The Holy Roman emperor Frederick II gained Jerusalem through diplomacy on the Sixth Crusade (1228–29), but the city was lost again in 1244. The Seventh Crusade (1248–54) under Louis IX of France was an exact repeat of the Fifth. The Eighth Crusade (1270), directed against Tunis, was a costly failure. Far more significant than the Crusades in ensuring the survival of the Crusader states in the 13th century were the Mongol attacks on the Muslim world. After decisively defeating the Mongols in 1260, the Mamlukes turned their full attention to the Crusader states, which fell in 1291.

Africa

The period from 600 to 1500 was a time in Africa of state and city building, increased trading, and the introduction of Islam.

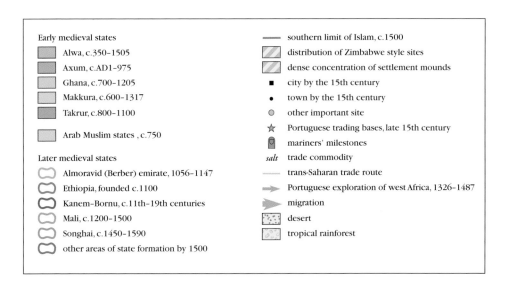

Early medieval states

- Alwa, c.350–1505
- Axum, c.AD1–975
- Ghana, c.700–1205
- Makkura, c.600–1317
- Takrur, c.800–1100

- Arab Muslim states , c.750

Later medieval states

- Almoravid (Berber) emirate, 1056–1147
- Ethiopia, founded c.1100
- Kanem–Bornu, c.11th–19th centuries
- Mali, c.1200–1500
- Songhai, c.1450–1590
- other areas of state formation by 1500

— southern limit of Islam, c.1500

▨ distribution of Zimbabwe style sites

▨ dense concentration of settlement mounds

■ city by the 15th century

• town by the 15th century

○ other important site

★ Portuguese trading bases, late 15th century

mariners' milestones

salt trade commodity

trans-Saharan trade route

Portuguese exploration of west Africa, 1326–1487

migration

desert

tropical rainforest

Tunis

Mediterranean Sea

Tripoli

adames

Alexandria

Cairo

Arabs

Ghat

Zuwaylah

SAHARA DESERT

Qusayr

ARABIA

Red Sea

Aswan

eg

Djado

salt

Bilma

Faras

Jiddah

Mecca

Arabs

Agadez

Ngarzagamu

Lake Chad

El Fasher

DARFUR

ivory

Suakin

NUBIA

Old Dongola

Berber

Dahlak

Danakil

atsina

Daima

Njimi

Kano

slaves

Soba

Dibarwa

Axum

salt

Aden

Saylac
1415

Ras
Xaafuun

FUNJ

Sennar

Lalibela

salt

Berbera

Agau

Debre Libanos

Harer

Somali

gold,
slaves

Debre Birhan

Dakar

ETHIOPIAN
HIGHLANDS

ADAL

Bernra

Oromo

Ukwu

Duala

Uele

CONGO
BASIN

Congo

White Nile

slaves

Nilotes

Lake
Turkana

RIFT VALLEY

Jasiira

Mogadishu

Baraawe

1472-82

Vili

Congo

Lulalaba

Lake
Victoria

Bigo

Ungwana

Shanga

Manda

Gedi

Malindi

ivory, slaves

Mombasa

INDIAN
OCEAN

Congo River

Mbanza Congo

CONGO

NDONGO

Lake
Tanganyika

Pemba Island

Zanzibar

1482

Sanga

Kikulu

Kamilamba

Mafia Island

Kalongo

Kilwa Kisiwani

Ovimbundu

Okavango

Lake
Malawi

ivory

Cape Sta Maria

Vohémar

East African Muslims

Shona

Zambezi

MWENEMUTAPA

Bantu speakers

Madagascar

Tonga

Malagasy

1482-85

Khami

gold

Great
Zimbabwe

Sofala

Tananarive

TORWA

Mapungubwe

Manekweni

Chibuene

Limpopo

1485-87

Angra Pequena

Kalahari
Desert

Orange

1487

Khoisan herders
and hunter
gatherers

Cape of Good Hope

Algoa Bay

1487

Cape Cross

Africa

In sub-Saharan Africa, the period 600–1500 witnessed the rise of chiefdoms, cities, states, and empires, so that by 1500 most Africans lived in complex societies of some sort. Islam, introduced by Arab merchants, also exerted a strong influence on west and east Africa from the 10th century onward.

Iron was in everyday use in sub-Saharan Africa by the 11th century and in west Africa, metalworkers made artifacts of high technical and artistic quality.

Early West African states

In the west African part of the Sahel (the southern fringe of the Sahara), state formation had begun by 600. The earliest known state, the kingdom of Ghana, had emerged by 700. Population growth and the development of regional trade routes in the early first millennium CE led to the growth of many large settlements along rivers and at waterholes before 600. The west African states grew out of amalgamations of smaller units—chiefdoms with populations of between 2,000 and 10,000 people, which dominated areas no more that 20–30 miles (30–50 km) across and were often centered on a single large settlement.

Mali and Songhai

Arising in the 13th century, the empire of Mali centered on fertile farmlands on the inland delta of the Niger River and controlled access to rich goldfields. Its government and army, which included a strong cavalry, were influenced by the Muslim states of north Africa. Cities such as Koumbi Saleh and Timbuktu at the southern end of the trans-Saharan camel caravan routes became centers where African slaves, ivory, and gold were exchanged for salt, cloth, glass, ceramics, horses, and other luxuries from the north. By 1500, Songhai, another cavalry state, was the chief west

African power. By 1300, small states such as Benin were developing in the forest regions of west Africa.

Southern African states

States had also begun to emerge in southern Africa by 1500. From about 1000 CE, many small chiefdoms had developed between the Zambezi and Limpopo rivers, where cattle formed the basis of the region's wealth. By the 13th century, Great Zimbabwe was dominant, its imposing stone architecture unequalled in sub-Saharan Africa at the time. Yet as power shifted north to the emerging state of Mwenemutapa in about 1450, Great Zimbabwe declined.

The east African coast

Trade was vital to the growth of city-states on the east African coast. These were founded by local Bantu-speaking peoples, perhaps to exploit existing trade links with the Mediterranean, West Asia, and India. Islam was brought by Arab merchants around 1000 CE. Despite strong cultural influence such as literacy and stone buildings, there was no large-scale Arab immigration.

Nubia and Ethiopia

The oldest states in sub-Saharan Africa in 600 were the Christian states in Nubia and Ethiopia. Makkura, the strongest Nubian state, conquered its neighbor Nobatia in the eighth century but fell to the Arabs in the 14th century. Another, Alwa, survived until 1505, when it was conquered by an alliance of Arabs and the southern Funj people. By 600, the Ethiopian kingdom of Axum was in decline, and the city of Axum was abandoned. The last traces of the state survived until 975. Christianity survived in the highlands. By the 12th century, the kingdom of Ethiopia had emerged around Lalibela. Under the Solomonid dynasty (1270–1777), Ethiopia expanded, bringing most of the Ethiopian highlands under its control by the 15th century and exacting tribute from its Muslim neighbors.

Curriculum Context

Many curricula ask students to explain the expansion of the Christian Ethiopian kingdom and its search for wider connections in the Christian world.

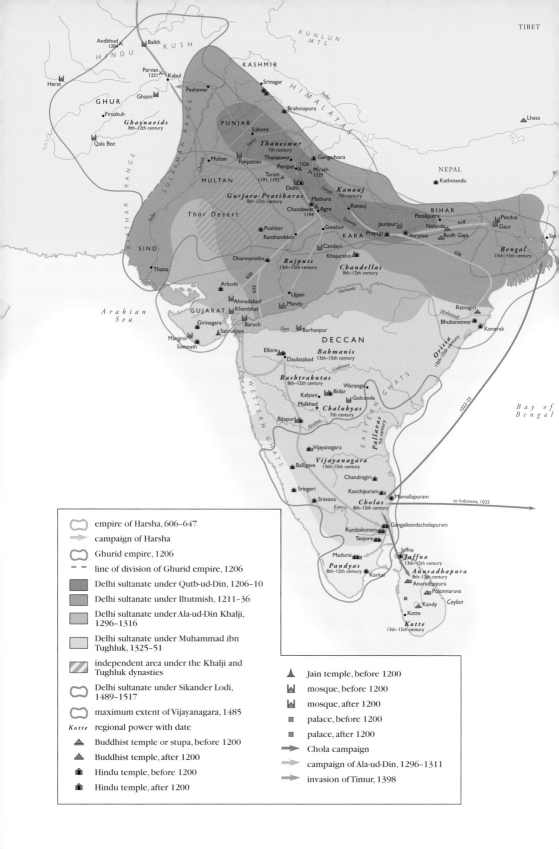

empire of Harsha, 606–647

campaign of Harsha

Ghurid empire, 1206

line of division of Ghurid empire, 1206

Delhi sultanate under Qutb-ud-Din, 1206–10

Delhi sultanate under Iltutmish, 1211–36

Delhi sultanate under Ala-ud-Din Khalji, 1296–1316

Delhi sultanate under Muhammad ibn Tughluk, 1325–51

independent area under the Khalji and Tughluk dynasties

Delhi sultanate under Sikander Lodi, 1489–1517

maximum extent of Vijayanagara, 1485

Kotte   regional power with date

Buddhist temple or stupa, before 1200

Buddhist temple, after 1200

Hindu temple, before 1200

Hindu temple, after 1200

Jain temple, before 1200

mosque, before 1200

mosque, after 1200

palace, before 1200

palace, after 1200

Chola campaign

campaign of Ala-ud-Din, 1296–1311

invasion of Timur, 1398

Medieval India

At the beginning of the seventh century, the most powerful Indian kingdom was Kanauj, which dominated the Gangetic plain. Shortly after ascending the throne of the minor kingdom of Thaneswar, Harsha also became king of Kanauj and began a career of conquest that united most of northern India under his rule.

However, Harsha's attempt to conquer the Deccan was defeated in 633 by the Chalukyas, the dominant power of central India. Harsha's empire fell apart after he was murdered in 647.

Regional wars, Buddhist revival

For the 600 years after the fall of Harsha's empire, the history of India was dominated by the rise and fall of regional kingdoms and short-lived dynasties. Regional wars were frequent; however, because the main kingdoms were roughly comparable in wealth, population, military strength, and tactics, a balance of power existed that precluded the formation of supraregional states. The period saw a strong revival of Hinduism and a commensurate decline of Buddhism throughout India with the exception of Ceylon (Sri Lanka). Hinduism also began to replace Buddhism in much of Southeast Asia, largely through the influence of the Tamil kingdom of the Cholas, a major mercantile and naval power.

The spread of Islam in India

The entire period from 700 to 1500 was dominated by the spread of Islam as a cultural and political force. Introduced into India by the Arabs, who conquered Sind and Multan in the early eighth century, Islam's advance under the Arabs was halted by the Gurjara-Pratiharas, a military Rajput dynasty that had become the main power in the north after the fall of Harsha's empire. However in 1000, the militant Muslim ruler

Curriculum Context

An exploration of how Hinduism responded to the challenges of Buddhism and prevailed as the dominant faith in India is included in many curricula.

Mercantile
Relating to trade or merchants.

Mahmud of Ghazni (r.999–1030) launched the first of his 17 invasions of India. Mahmud broke the power of the Gurjara-Pratiharas and the Chandellas but only incorporated the Punjab into his empire. His main concern was with plunder and with despoiling Hindu temples. After Mahmud's death, the Ghaznavid emirate declined; for 150 years, there was no further Islamic advance in India. In 1151, the Ghaznavids were overthrown by the governor of Ghur. From 1175 onward, Muhammad of Ghur (r.1173–1206) made a concerted effort to conquer northern India. Following his victory over a confederation of Rajput rulers at the second battle of Tarain in 1192, Hindu resistance began to crumble. By 1200, he was master of the Indus and Gangetic plains and had laid the foundations for 600 years of Muslim dominance in India.

Confederation
An alliance.

Muslim strength, Hindu weakness

Muhammad of Ghur's victory was the result of both Muslim strength and Hindu weakness. The Muslim army was a professional force of disciplined and highly mobile horse archers. Many Muslim soldiers were slaves, who were trained for battle from childhood, but a military career was open to all—unlike in the Hindu states—and rapid advancement was possible for anyone who showed ability, whether they were enslaved or free. Also, the Muslim army was invading a country rich in plunder and its soldiers were further motivated by religious fervor.

The Delhi sultanate

On the death of Muhammad in 1206, the Turkish slave-general Qutb-ud-Din broke away from the Ghurid empire, founding an independent sultanate at Delhi. Qutb-ud-Din faced widespread Hindu rebellions, but his successor Iltutmish (r.1211–36) consolidated the Muslim conquest of northern India. Qutb-ud-Din's dynasty was overthrown in 1290 by the Khalji dynasty (1290–1320). Under the second Khalji ruler, Ala-ud-Din, the sultanate's control was extended south of the Narmada River in the Deccan. The sultanate reached its of government to the massive hilltop fortress of Daulatabad in central India but, by moving away from Delhi, he lost control of the north while failing to consolidate his hold on the south. Muhammad was forced to return to Delhi to restore order, leaving the Deccan in the charge of a governor, Hasan Gungu, who revolted in 1347 to establish the independent Bahmani sultanate.

Hindu and Muslim states

At the same time, the Hindu kingdom of Vijayanagara started to establish itself as a substantial military and political power in the south. New lessons of warfare were learned from the Muslims, and full-time armies equipped with horses and elephants were raised and paid for. Further Muslim expansion into the Deccan was halted and, by the end of the 15th century, the Bahmani kingdom had fragmented into five independent sultanates.

After 1388, the Delhi sultanate rapidly began to lose its hold over its northern provinces, a process completed by Timur the Lame's sacking of Delhi in 1398. Decline continued under the Sayyid dynasty (1414–51) until the sultanate was reduced to Delhi and its hinterland. Despite the collapse of the sultanate, northern and central India remained under Muslim control. Only in parts of Gujarat, Kara, Orissa, and the south, where the kingdom of Vijayanagara reigned supreme, were there independent Hindu states. Under the Lodis (1451–1526), a dynasty from Afghanistan, the Delhi sultanate recovered control of the Punjab and the Gangetic plain once again to achieve domination over northern India. However, the recovery was short-lived and, in 1526, the sultanate was destroyed by Babur, founder of the Mughal empire.

Hinterland
A region beyond an urban center.

Sui and Tang China

The Sui and Tang dynasties ruled China between 589 and 907 CE, a period in which the peasantry became more prosperous and trade flourished.

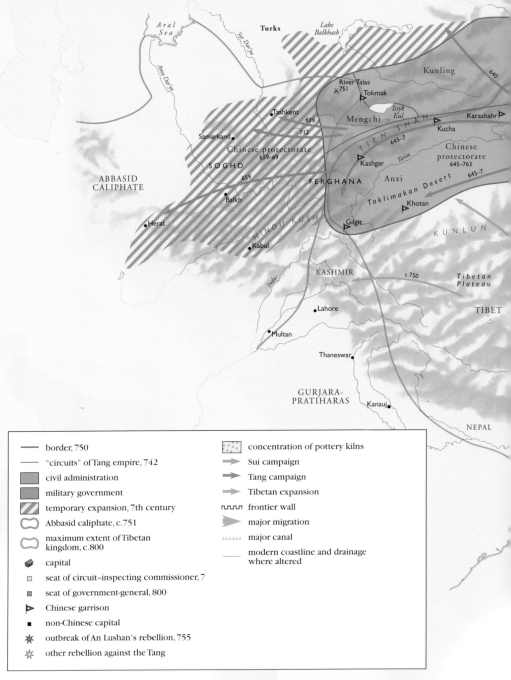

Aral Sea

Turks

Lake Balkhash

Kunling

640

Syr Dar'ya

Amu Dar'ya

River Talas ×751

Tokmak

Issyk Kul

Tashkent

659

Mengchi

Karashahr

712

Kucha

Samarkand

TIEN SHAN

645–7

Chinese protectorate

Kashgar

Tarim

Chinese protectorate 645–763

659–69

SOGHD

Anxi

645–7

659

FERGHANA

Taklimakan Desert

ABBASID CALIPHATE

Balkh

Khotan

HINDU KUSH

Gilgit

KUNLUN

Herat

Kabul

KASHMIR

c.750

Tibetan Plateau

Lahore

TIBET

Multan

Thaneswar

GURJARA-PRATIHARAS

Kanauj

NEPAL

Legend

border, 750	concentration of pottery kilns
"circuits" of Tang empire, 742	Sui campaign
civil administration	Tang campaign
military government	Tibetan expansion
temporary expansion, 7th century	frontier wall
Abbasid caliphate, c.751	major migration
maximum extent of Tibetan kingdom, c.800	major canal
capital	modern coastline and drainage where altered
seat of circuit-inspecting commissioner, 7	
seat of government-general, 800	
Chinese garrison	
non-Chinese capital	
outbreak of An Lushan's rebellion, 755	
other rebellion against the Tang	

Karabalghasun

Uighurs

Inner Mongolian Plateau

Gobi Desert

Khitans

KOGURYO
Chinese protectorate 668–76
645–7, 660–6

ALTAI MTS

Tingzhou
791

Yingzhou

611–614

Pyongyang

You
Jojun
(Beijing)

630

660

Kyongju

SILLA

Anxi
Gansu Corridor
607–9

Dunhuang
Suzhou

QILIAN MTS

Liang

Shan

Lake Qinghai

787

791

763

Feng
Sheng
Yun

Hebei

Yellow

874

Henan

Yellow Sea

Yan
Ling

Hedong
Taiyuan

Heng
Wei

Yellow river (891–1048)

Yan

Guannei
Qing

Pu
Shan
Luoyang

Bianzhou

Yangzhou

Yuan

Wei
Qin
Jingji
Chang'an

Duji
Caizhou

Shouzou

Su

Yue
859

Longyou

Liang

Han

Huainan

Song
Li

Shanan-Xi
Shanan-Dong

Kui

An

Jiannan

Chengdu

Qian

Hong
(Nanchang)

Jiangnan-Dong

Tibetans

Ya

Tanzhou

Fu

620–50

Lhasa

Brahmaputra

Li

Qianzhong
868

Jiangnan-Xi

610

Taiwan

MALAYAS

Mekong

Sui

Yaozhou

751

607–10

Gui

Dali
751
Longyu

NAN CHAO

Lingnan

Guangzhou

Red

Yong

Rong

602–5

PYU

Salween

Irrawaddy

Han

Qiongzhou

Hainan

Annam

Mekong

CHAMPA

Indrapura

Sui and Tang China

The centralized Chinese empire created by Shi Huangdi survived until 220 CE, when it split into three rival states. Unity was restored in 589 by Yang Jian, who as emperor Wen (r.589–604) became the founder of the Sui dynasty.

Wen reestablished a strong centralized bureaucracy and increased the prosperity of the peasantry through a land redistribution scheme. Granaries were built, and the canal system expanded. As a result of Wen's reforms, the economy grew rapidly, and the state amassed large reserves of cash and commodities. These were squandered by Wen's successor Yang (r.604–17) on building projects and opulent court life. Moreover, a disastrous war against the Korean kingdom of Koguryo caused the peasants of the northeast to rebel. The empire was saved by the coup of Li Yuan, military governor of Taiyuan, who captured the Sui capital at Luoyang in 617 and became, after Yang's murder in 618, the first emperor of the Tang dynasty (as Gaozong, r.618–26). Gaozong was then deposed by his son Taizong (r.626–49), one of China's ablest rulers.

Tang government

Taizong based his government loosely on the Han model but without the feudal elements. At its head was the emperor, whose authority was absolute. The central administration consisted of three bodies: the Imperial Chancellery, the Imperial Secretariat, and the Department for State Affairs. This latter department supervised the six ministries—officials, finances, religious rites, the army, justice, and public works. A Board of Censors oversaw the actions of officials.

The empire was divided into 15 administrative regions, or "circuits," under an inspecting commissioner. The examination system became more important for selecting bureaucratic staff, yet the cost of education

Curriculum Context

Many curricula ask students to describe the political centralization and economic reforms that marked China's reunification under the Sui and Tang dynasties.

precluded all but the rich landowning classes from pursuing a career in administration.

The peasantry benefited from further land redistribution and reduced tax and labor dues, and agricultural production rose rapidly. Internal trade flourished, stimulating craft production: silks and ceramics were widely exported.

Tang expansion

Taizong began to extend Chinese control into central Asia, creating a military protectorate in the Tarim basin. This expansion brought the first extensive contacts between China and Tibet, which had emerged as a powerful centralized kingdom. In the east, the Chinese subdued Koguryo in 668, but the Korean kingdom of Silla expelled them in 676.

Tang decline

The Chinese position in central Asia was dealt further blows in 751, with defeats by the Arabs at the Talas River and by the Thai kingdom of Nan Chao at Dali. The Mongol Khitan nomads emerged as a threat in the north in the eighth century. A rebellion led by An Lushan in 755 threatened the Tang; it was suppressed in 763, but central authority did not recover, and power devolved to around 40 semi-independent military governments-general. In 859, 868, and 874–84, peasant rebellions broke out. The emperor's authority was damaged beyond repair, and power was seized by provincial warlords. The Tang struggled on until 907, finally collapsing in a period of disunity known as the Five Dynasties and Ten Kingdoms (907–960).

The Tang period is regarded as the golden age of Chinese poetry. The dynasty also presided over major achievements in historiography and painting, and restored Confucianism as the state ideology after it had declined during the Period of Disunion.

Protectorate
A state that is dependent on or under the authority of another.

Curriculum Context

Describing Tang imperial conquests in Southeast and Central Asia helps students understand patterns of historical succession and duration.

Historiography
Writing about history.

Song China

The Song dynasty ruled China from 960 to 1279, a period of territorial losses but economic prosperity.

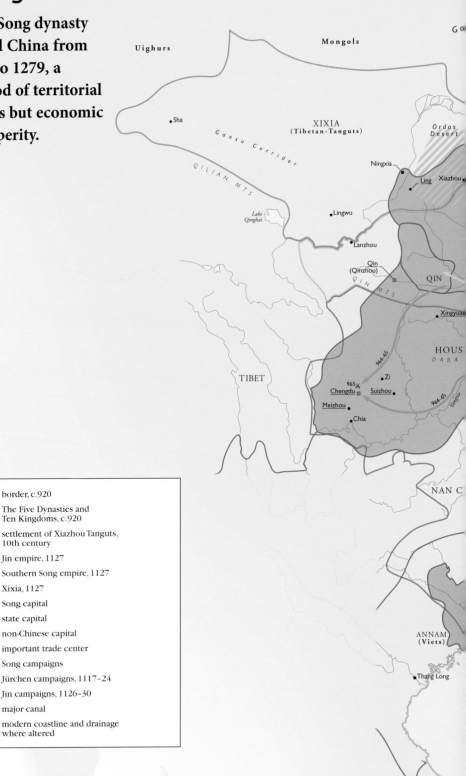

Uighurs

Mongols

Go

Sha

XIXIA
(Tibetan-Tanguts)

Ordos Desert

Gansu Corridor

Ningxia

Ling   Xiazhou

QILIAN MTS

Lake Qinghai

Lingwu

Lanzhou

Qin
(Qinzhou)

QIN

QIN

MTS

Xingyua

TIBET

964-65

HOUS
DABA

965   Zi

Chengdu   Suizhou

Meizhou

964-65

Yangtze

Chia

NAN C

ANNAM
(Viets)

Thang Long

——	border, c.920
▨	The Five Dynasties and Ten Kingdoms, c.920
▨	settlement of Xiazhou Tanguts, 10th century
◖◗	Jin empire, 1127
◖◗	Southern Song empire, 1127
◖◗	Xixia, 1127
⬢	Song capital
▪	state capital
▪	non-Chinese capital
Su	important trade center
➤	Song campaigns
➤	Jürchen campaigns, 1117–24
➤	Jin campaigns, 1126–30
⊔⊔⊔	major canal
——	modern coastline and drainage where altered

Jürchen

Linhuang
Liao capital

LIAO
(Khitans)

Dading
Jin capital

PARHAE

Liaoyang

Datong

Sanggan

979 Xijin
(Beijing)

YEN

Zongdu

JIN

Dingzhou

1115-22

979

Taiyuan

Fen

Dengzhou

Qingzhou

Mi

Daming

Yellow river (1048-1194)

Ji (present day Yellow river)

KOREA

Kaegyong

Yellow
Sea

Luoyang

Ying

Kaifeng
Northern
Song capital

THE FIVE
DYNASTIES

Lake
Hongze

Huai'an

Huai

Shouzou

Zaishi
1161

Yangzhou

Nanjing

Han

963

Xiangyang

Lu

Changzhou

Su

Lake
Tai

Hu

974-75

AN

Jiangling

Huanggang

975

Yangzi

Lizhou
963

Yuezhou

Jiangzhou

963

Longxing
(Nanchang)

Lake
Pengli

WU

Lake
Dongting

Tanzhou

964

Jizhou

Hangzhou
Southern
Song capital

Ningbo

Qu

WUYUE

Wenzhou

Fuzhou

MIN

Taiwan

970

CHU

SOUTHERN HAN

Nanxiang
970

Guangzhou

Yaishan
1279

Qiongzhou

South
China
Sea

Hainan

Song China

The disunity of the Five Dynasties and Ten Kingdoms period began to come to an end when Song Taizu (r.960–76) overthrew the last of the Five Dynasties, which had ruled the Yellow River valley since 907, in a military coup.

Taizu brought the military under civilian political control. In 963, he began a series of diplomatic and military campaigns to reunify China. This process was completed by his equally able brother Song Taizong (r.976–97), so creating the third Chinese empire. Only in Taiyuan, which had the support of the nomadic Khitans, and Houshu did the Song meet determined resistance. However, the Song were not able to restore the borders of the Tang empire, and their authority was confined to areas of ethnic Chinese settlement. Unlike the Tang, the Song empire was surrounded by well-organized states that blocked Chinese expansion.

The Khitans and the Jin

The most powerful of these states was the Khitan Liao kingdom. The Khitans were a Turko-Mongol nomadic people, who had won control of the northern Chinese plains in 916 and went on to dominate the eastern steppes. Taizong attempted to drive the Khitans back to the steppes in 979 but was badly defeated near Beijing. A Khitan attack on the Song capital Kaifeng in 1004 was bought off by a heavy annual tribute of silver, silk, and tea and, thereafter, relations between Song and Liao were peaceful. The Khitans adopted Chinese administrative practices to govern their kingdom and by the end of the 11th century they had become thoroughly assimilated. In 1114, the Jürchen people of Manchuria broke off payments of tribute to the Khitans and three years later launched an invasion of Liao, which collapsed in 1124. The Jürchen created their own state under the Jin dynasty and, in 1127, the Jin captured Kaifeng, forcing the Song dynasty to

Tribute
Payment by one state to another for protection or to indicate submission.

withdraw south to Hangzhou. Because of population shifts over the preceding centuries, the loss of the north did not cripple the Song. The south now had the majority of China's population and wealth, so the Song remained strong enough to keep the Jin at bay. They made no attempt to reconquer the north from the Jin.

Xixia

A more serious obstacle to Chinese expansion was the kingdom of Xixia. It dominated the Gansu corridor, shutting the Song out of central Asia. Xixia was founded in the late 10th century by a clan of the nomadic Tangut people. With a mixed Tangut, Tibetan, and Chinese population, it never became as sinicized as Liao. In the south, the Thai kingdom of Nan Chao and the Viet kingdom of Annam blocked expansion.

Mongol attacks

The Mongol steppe nomads were unified at the beginning of the 13th century by Chingis Khan, who then turned on Xixia and Jin. The Song refused appeals by Jin for help and even supplied the Mongols with troops. When the Song tried to profit from the fall of Jin in 1234 by seizing Kaifeng and Luoyang, the Mongols turned on them. Song resistance to the Mongols collapsed after the capture of Hangzhou in 1276. The last Song emperor drowned three years later.

Song achievements

The Song are regarded as one of the most capable and humane dynasties in Chinese history. The Song period was one of economic prosperity, technological innovation, and rapid population growth. Agricultural productivity was increased by the introduction of Vietnamese strains of rice in the 12th century. External and internal trade flourished, and government income from dues on trade exceeded that from land taxes. Banking and paper money were introduced.

Sinicized
Changed by Chinese influence.

Curriculum Context
Improved agricultural production, population growth, urbanization, and commercialization were interconnected in China between the 10th and 13th centuries.

The Mongol Empire

The Mongols were peoples of the Asian steppes who joined together, formed a cavalry army, and conquered a vast empire in Asia and Europe between 1206 and 1260.

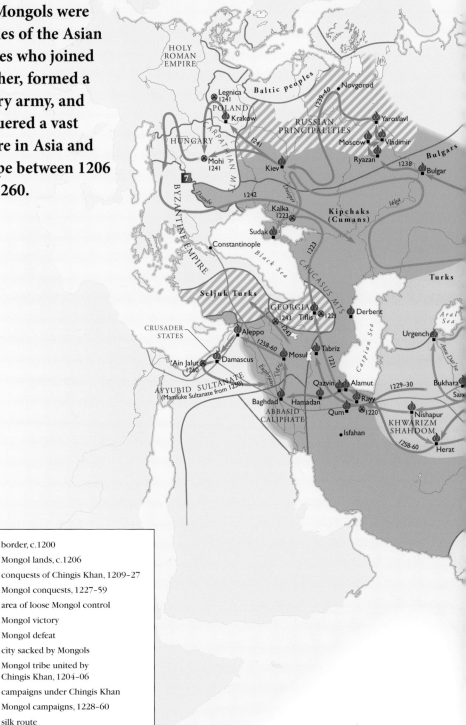

HOLY ROMAN EMPIRE

Baltic peoples

POLAND
Legnica 1241
Krakow

HUNGARY

Mohi 1241

Kiev

BYZANTINE EMPIRE

Danube

Constantinople

Black Sea

Seljuk Turks

CRUSADER STATES

Aleppo

'Ain Jalut 1260
Damascus

AYYUBID SULTANATE
(Mamluke Sultanate from 1250)

Baghdad
Hamadan

ABBASID CALIPHATE

Isfahan

RUSSIAN PRINCIPALITIES
1239–40
Novgorod

Yaroslavl
Moscow
Vladimir
Ryazan
1238
Bulgar

Bulgars

1241

1242

Kalka 1223

Sudak

Kipchaks (Cumans)

Volga

CAUCASUS MTS

1223

GEORGIA
1243 Tiflis 1221
Derbent

Turks

Aral Sea

Urgench

Tabriz
Mosul
1221

Qazvin
Alamut
1229–30
Bukhara
San
Qum 1220
Rayy

Nishapur
KHWARIZM SHAHDOM

1258–60
Herat

Amu Darya

Caspian Sea

1258–60

Tigris

Euphrates

Legend:

— border, c.1200
▨ Mongol lands, c.1206
▨ conquests of Chingis Khan, 1209–27
▨ Mongol conquests, 1227–59
▨ area of loose Mongol control
⊗ Mongol victory
⊗ Mongol defeat
♨ city sacked by Mongols
TATARS Mongol tribe united by Chingis Khan, 1204–06
➤ campaigns under Chingis Khan
➤ Mongol campaigns, 1228–60
— silk route

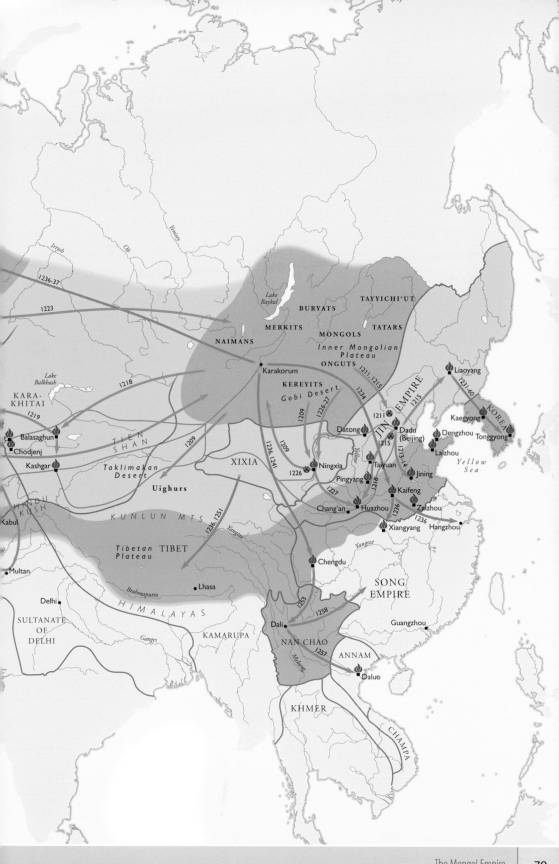

Iryah

Ob

Yenisey

1236-37

1223

Lake
Baykal

BURYATS

TAYYICHI'UT

MERKITS

MONGOLS

TATARS

NAIMANS

Inner Mongolian
Plateau

ONGUTS

Karakorum

1211, 1215

Liaoyang

1231-60

Lake
Balkhash

1218

KEREYITS

Gobi Desert

1234

1211

JIN EMPIRE

1215

Kaegyong

KOREA

KARA-
KHITAI

1219

TIEN
SHAN

1209

1226-27

Datong

1215

Dadu
(Beijing)

Dengzhou

Tonggyong

Balasaghun

Chodjenj

1218

1209

Taiyuan

1213-14

Laizhou

Yellow
Sea

Kashgar

Taklimakan
Desert

XIXIA

1209

1226

Ningxia

Pingyang

1218

Jining

Uighurs

1236, 1241

Kaifeng

KUNLUN MTS.

1227

Chang'an

Huazhou

1236

Zaizhou

HINDU
KUSH

Kabul

Tibetan
Plateau

TIBET

1236, 1251

Yangtze

Xiangyang

1236

Hangzhou

Multan

Lhasa

Brahmaputra

Chengdu

Yangtze

SONG
EMPIRE

Delhi

HIMALAYAS

Ganges

1253

SULTANATE
OF
DELHI

KAMARUPA

Dali

NAN CHAO

1258

Guangzhou

1257

ANNAM

Daluo

KHMER

Mekong

CHAMPA

The Mongol Empire

The dramatic expansion of the Mongols that began under Temujin was the most important event in world history in the 13th century. The son of a minor Mongol chief, Temujin displayed brilliant leadership in intertribal warfare that enabled him to unify the Mongol peoples in a ruthless two-year campaign.

To mark his success he was proclaimed Chingis ("universal") Khan in 1206. During his unification campaign, he created the finest cavalry army that the world has ever seen. If the army was not to break up, and his khandom with it, he had to find work for it to do and wealth with which to reward it. By his death in 1227, he had conquered an empire that included most of central Asia and northern China. His successors carried the Mongol conquests into Europe and West Asia. In China, only the southern Song empire stood out against the Mongols for a time.

Disunited enemies

The Mongol conquests formed the largest land empire in history. The achievement is all the more remarkable because the Mongols had few governmental institutions and did not even possess basic metalworking skills. They were able to exploit disunity among their enemies: China was divided into three hostile kingdoms; the Turkish empires of Kara-Khitai and Khwarizm were mutually hostile; and Russia was a mosaic of quarrelsome states.

The Mongol army

The key factor in the Mongol success, however, was the magnificent army that Chingis created. Promotion in the Mongol army was by merit only. The discipline and mobility of the Mongol army enabled it to execute complex battlefield maneuvers. A frequent tactic was the feigned retreat, used to lure rash pursuers into

Khandom
State ruled by a khan.

Curriculum Context

Assessing the career of Chingis Khan as a conqueror and military innovator in the context of Mongol society helps students understand the importance of the individual in history.

ambushes on unfavorable ground, where they could be destroyed. The Mongols had an excellent long-range weapon in the composite bow, which enabled them to inflict casualties while keeping out of danger themselves. The Mongols also committed horrific atrocities, systematically creating terror to sap their enemies' will to resist.

Mongol limitations

Except in China, the boundaries of the Mongol empire were very close to those of the Eurasian steppes and grasslands, which alone could provide the necessary grazing for the vast herds of horses that accompanied every Mongol army. The defeat suffered by the Mongols at the hands of the Mamlukes at 'Ain Jalut in 1260 was to some extent the result of poor grazing in the Syrian desert. This was probably also the reason why the Mongols never returned to Europe after their invasion of 1241–42. The army also needed plenty of room for maneuver, so it was least effective in forested, mountainous, or intensively farmed areas.

Mongol impact

The period of the Mongols' expansion had few beneficial results. The Abbasid caliphate of Baghdad was overthrown. The ancient cities of central Asia were devastated and never recovered their former prosperity. Depopulation and neglect of irrigation channels meant that most of Iraq and west Persia were reduced to desert for centuries. Northern China suffered depopulation, and Russia was isolated from the mainstream of European development for almost two centuries. By disrupting the Muslim world, the Mongols briefly saved the Crusader States and allowed a shortlived revival of the crumbling Byzantine empire. Christendom benefited from Mongol conquests in Asia, as Muslim control of the Silk Road ended, and the way was opened for westerners such as Marco Polo to travel to eastern Asia for the first time.

The Break-up of the Mongol Empire

After 1260, the Mongol Empire split up into smaller states that had ceased to exist by 1502.

Mongol territory at the death of Möngke Khan, 1259

tributary area, 1259

conquered by Khubilai Khan, 1268–79

border, 1280

area of origin of the Ming dynasty

Ming empire, c.1400

Ottoman Turk empire, 1402

empire of Timur, 1405

Mongol victory

Mongol defeat

Mongol versus Mongol

city sacked by Timur the Lame

Mongol capital, 1259–1405

Khubilai Khan's conquest of the Song empire, 1268–79

late campaign of Khubilai Khan

other Mongol campaign

campaign of Timur the Lame, 1369–1405

route of Marco Polo, 1271–95

Ming dynasty frontier wall

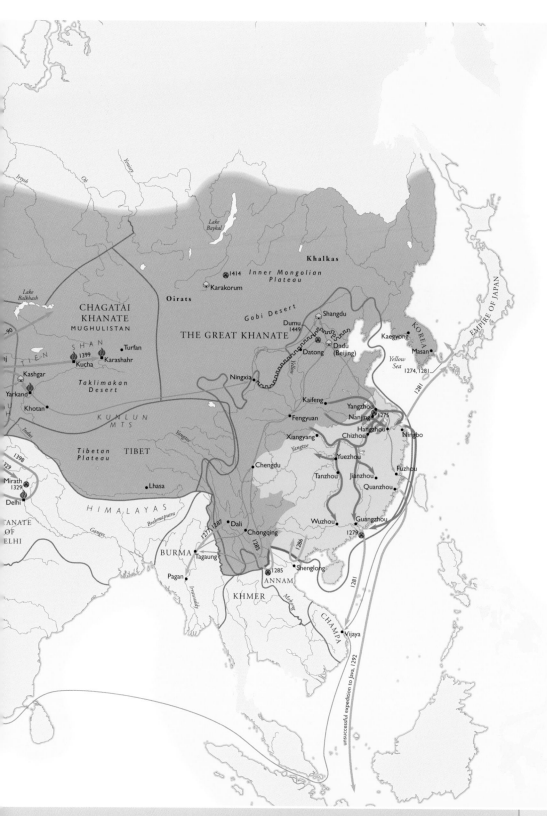

Irtysh

Ob

Yenisei

Lake Baykal

Khalkas

⊗1414
Karakorum

Inner Mongolian Plateau

Oirats

Lake Balkhash

CHAGATAI KHANATE

MUGHULISTAN

Gobi Desert

Shangdu

Dumu 1449

Kaegyong

KOREA

EMPIRE OF JAPAN

90

T I E N S H A N

1399
Kucha ●Turfan
Karashahr

THE GREAT KHANATE

Datong

Dadu (Beijing)

Masan

Yellow Sea

1274, 1281

Kashgar

Taklimakan Desert

Ningxia

1281

Yarkand

Khotan●

K U N L U N M T S

Yangtze

Kaifeng

Fengyuan●

Yangzhou
Nanjing● 1275
Hangzhou
Chizhou
Ningbo

U

1398

Tibetan Plateau

TIBET

Xiangyang●

Yangtze

Yuezhou

Fuzhou

Indus

729

Chengdu●

Tanzhou● Jianzhou

Quanzhou

Mirath 1329

●Lhasa

Delhi

H I M A L A Y A S

Brahmaputra

Wuzhou●

Guangzhou

Ganges

1277 1287

●Dali

Chongqing

1285

1286

1279

ANATE OF ELHI

BURMA

●Tagaung

1285

Shenglong

Pagan●

Irrawaddy

ANNAM

KHMER

Mekong

CHAMPA

1281

Vijaya●

unsuccessful expedition to Java, 1292

The Break-up of the Mongol Empire

The empire created by Chingis Khan was too vast to be ruled by one man. In the reigns of his successors, Ogedai (r.1229–41) and Möngke (r.1251–59), subordinate khanates were created to govern the western conquests. After Möngke's death, the western khanates became fully independent states, and Khubilai (r.1260–94), his successor, had a purely nominal sovereignty over them.

Curriculum Context

Many curricula ask students to describe the Mongol conquests of 1206–1279 and assess their effects on peoples of China, Southeast Asia, Russia, and Southwest Asia.

Khubilai's conquest of the Song empire in 1268–79 ended the period of Mongol conquests. His attempts at expansion in Southeast Asia and Japan failed.

Chinese successes

Khubilai's successors as Great Khan were all mediocrities, who failed to give their empire a stable centralized administration. Peasant rebellions became common in the 14th century and, by 1355, the Great Khanate had broken up into separate states. A Chinese rebel leader, Zhu Yuanzhang, seized control of Nanjing in 1356, and by 1367, won control of southern China. In 1368, Zhu recaptured Beijing and declared himself the first emperor of the Ming dynasty (1368–1644). The early Ming emperors refortified the northern frontier and launched frequent campaigns into Mongolia.

Chinese isolation

Trade and cultural contacts between China and the rest of the world increased greatly under Mongol rule. Many European missionaries and merchants—most famously the Venetian Marco Polo—found their way to China, taking home with them the first detailed accounts of Chinese civilization. Although the Christian and Islamic worlds benefited from these cultural contacts, China itself did not. Most trade was controlled by foreigners, and currency drained out of China. The painful experience of Mongol rule seemed to the Chinese to vindicate their ancient xenophobia and

Xenophobia

Fear or hatred of foreigners.

sense of cultural superiority. When Mongol rule ended, they unwisely renounced all foreign influences, just as China was losing its economic and technological lead.

Mongol khanates

The Ilkhanate of Persia, founded in 1256, lasted only until 1335 despite a series of able rulers. By 1300, most Mongols had converted to Islam. On the death of the last khan, the Ilkhanate split into several Mongol, Turkish, and Persian states.

The steppe khanates of the Golden Horde and the Chagatai, where the Mongols could pursue their traditional way of life, survived the longest. The population of the Golden Horde was mainly Turkish: they adopted Turkish as the official language in about 1280 and Islam in the early 14th century. The Chagatai khanate was divided into an eastern area dominated by paganism and nomadism and a western area dominated by the great Muslim cities of the Silk Road. Antagonism between them was exploited by the last Mongol conqueror, Timur the Lame (r.1361–1405).

Curriculum Context

Students should be able to explain the growth of the kingdom of the Golden Horde and its impact on the peoples of Russia, Ukraine, Poland, and Hungary.

Timur the Lame

Timur was a Muslim, and culturally and linguistically Turkish. He was appointed emir of Samarkand in 1361 and established a power base in Transoxiana by organizing defenses against nomad raiders from Mughulistan. In 1370, he captured Balkh, murdered its ruler, and massacred its populace. Timur spent the rest of his life in almost constant campaigning, yet the empire he built died with him. His campaigns were marked by appalling savagery and widespread plundering. A militant Muslim, he left the Islamic world in ruins; moreover, although claiming to restore Chingis Khan's empire, he weakened the Golden Horde and the Chagatai khanate. The Chagatai khanate was reduced to the lands around Kashgar. The Golden Horde split up in 1438, disappearing in 1502.

Medieval Japan and Korea

Both Japan and Korea attempted to build centralized states between 600 and 1500 CE, but in Japan, provincial warlords created a feudal system.

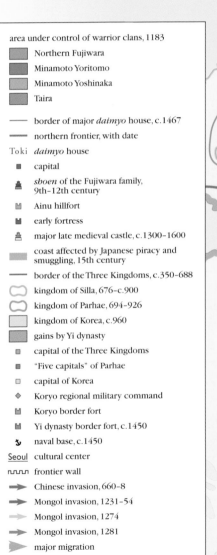

area under control of warrior clans, 1183

- Northern Fujiwara
- Minamoto Yoritomo
- Minamoto Yoshinaka
- Taira

— border of major *daimyo* house, c.1467

— northern frontier, with date

Toki *daimyo* house

■ capital

⚱ *shoen* of the Fujiwara family, 9th–12th century

🏯 Ainu hillfort

🏯 early fortress

⚱ major late medieval castle, c.1300–1600

▬ coast affected by Japanese piracy and smuggling, 15th century

— border of the Three Kingdoms, c.350–688

◗ kingdom of Silla, 676–c.900

◗ kingdom of Parhae, 694–926

▢ kingdom of Korea, c.960

■ gains by Yi dynasty

■ capital of the Three Kingdoms

■ "Five capitals" of Parhae

□ capital of Korea

◆ Koryo regional military command

🏯 Koryo border fort

🏯 Yi dynasty border fort, c.1450

⚓ naval base, c.1450

Seoul cultural center

〰 frontier wall

➤ Chinese invasion, 660–8

➤ Mongol invasion, 1231–54

➤ Mongol invasion, 1274

➤ Mongol invasion, 1281

➤ major migration

Jürchen
(pastoral farmers)

Khanka

12th century

nggyong

Sakhalin

Ainu
(hunter–gatherers)

Hokkaido

c 1000

Ezo

Nie

Akita
Yokote
Mogami
Ogachi
Tamatsukuri
Taga
Date
Atsugashiyama
1189

c 800
Esashi
Izawa

*Sea of
Japan*

Sado

Tsukahara

c 600
Wakamatsu

*PACIFIC
OCEAN*

Echigo
Hatakeyama
Kanazawa
Matsumoto

Uesugi
Shinano

Ashikaga
Tone

Ashikaga

Satake

Oki

Shiba
Toki
Gifu
Inuyama
Imagawa

Kamakura
Edo
Kanazawa

Akamatsu
Izumo
Yamana
Kyogoku
Himeji
Okayama
Komatsu

Heian
(Kyoto)
Nijo
Osaka
Sakai
Nara
Isshiki

Ise

Hamamatsu

Sumpu
Odawara
1333

Honshu

Ouchi
Yamaguchi
oura
1185
Hakataka Bay
1281
Hososhima

Takeda

Hosokawa

Hatakeyama

Kumano

Hiraoka

Shikoku

Veifu
Otomo

Shimazu

*Osumi
Islands*

Medieval Japan and Korea

By 600 CE, Chinese administrative practices and political ideologies were being introduced by Japanese and Korean rulers as they attempted to build centralized states. These endeavors had been largely successful in Korea by the 15th century. In Japan, initial success was followed by decentralization of authority and, in the 15th century, the growth of feudalism.

In Japan, attempts to build a centralized state began when Prince Shotoku (r.593–622) introduced a constitution asserting the power of the emperor over the nobility.

Japanese reforms

The reforms that followed in 646 brought all land into imperial ownership and instituted a tax system. In 702, the Taiho laws—new civil and penal codes—were introduced and in 710, a permanent administrative capital was established at Nara.

Buddhist monasteries and aristocratic houses

Nara became an important religious center, and the Buddhist clergy soon began to exert strong political influence over the emperors. To escape this interference, Emperor Kammu moved the court to a new capital at Heian (modern Kyoto) in 794. Here the aristocratic Fujiwara family married into the imperial family. Buddhist monasteries and great families such as the Fujiwara amassed extensive landholdings at imperial expense. They formed private armies, and a class of rural warriors—the *samurai*—developed.

Warriors and warlords

In the 12th century, samurai clans became involved in court politics, and Fujiwara influence declined. At the end of the 12th century, Minamoto Yoritomo founded the Kamakura shogunate, which was overthrown in

Clergy
The priestly class, or priesthood, in a state.

Curriculum Context

Many curricula ask students to describe the establishment of the imperial state in Japan and assess the role of the emperor in government.

1333 and replaced five years later by the Ashikaga shogunate. The shoguns ruled in alliance with the *shugo* (military constables), who gradually became powerful regional rulers. During a civil war between 1467 and 1477, the shugo lost control of their regional power bases. Control of the provinces fell to new feudal warlords, or *daimyo*, who feuded among themselves, deploying armies of samurai vassals who held small estates in return for military service. By 1500, Japan had fragmented into almost 400 effectively independent states. The emperors continued to reign in Heian but were powerless.

Korean kingdoms

In Korea, three kingdoms—Koguryo, Silla, and Paekche—had emerged by 600. In 660, the Chinese Tang dynasty invaded the peninsula and, in alliance with Silla, conquered Paekche and Koguryo. On finding that it was not to share in the spoils, Silla drove the Chinese from the peninsula in 676 and occupied Paekche and southern Koguryo. Northern Koguryo remained in chaos until a successor state, Parhae, emerged in 694. In 780, a struggle between the monarchy and the aristocracy broke out in Silla and in the ninth century, the kingdom broke up. A new kingdom was created by Wang Kon (r.918–45), founder of the Koryo dynasty. Parhae was extinguished about the same time by the Khitan nomads.

The military Choe family seized power in 1196. The Choe led resistance to the Mongols, but the dynasty was overthrown in 1258, and Korea became a Mongol vassal state. The end of Mongol rule in 1356 brought political instability, and the Koryo dynasty was eventually overthrown with Chinese help by the general Yi Songgye, founder of the Yi dynasty (1392–1910). Under the Yi, Confucianism replaced Buddhism as Korea's main ethical code and was made the basis of the bureaucratic and educational systems.

Shogunate

A Japanese state under military government, led by a shogun.

Curriculum Context

Explaining how Korea assimilated Chinese ideas and institutions yet preserved its political independence helps students to compare and contrast different sets of ideas.

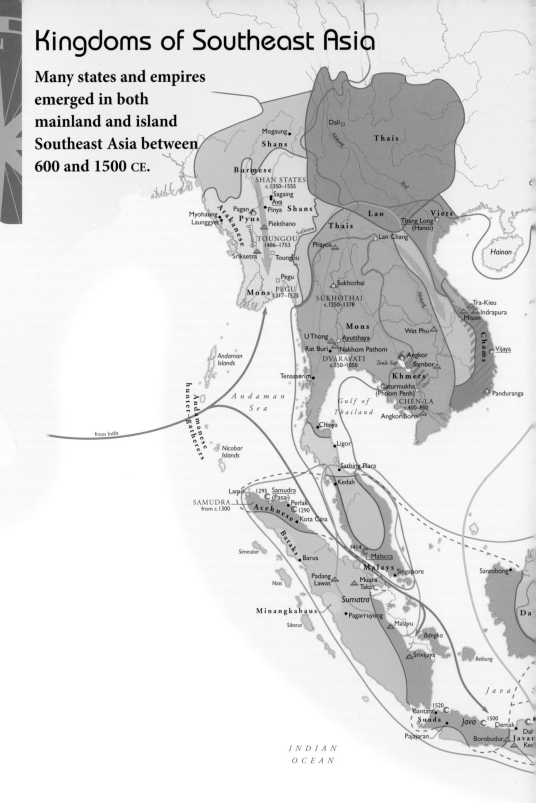

Kingdoms of Southeast Asia

Many states and empires emerged in both mainland and island Southeast Asia between 600 and 1500 CE.

Dali

Thais

Mogaung

Shans

Burmese

SHAN STATES
c.1350–1555

Sagaing

Ava

Pinya

Shans

Lao

Viets

Pagan

Thang Long
(Hanoi)

Myohaung
Launggyet

Pyus

Piekthano

Lan Chang

Hainan

Arakanese

Phayoa

Thais

Sriksetra

TOUNGOU
1486–1753

Toungou

Sukhothai

Tra-Kieu

Indrapura

Mison

Pegu

Mons

PEGU
1317–1535

SUKHOTHAI
c.1250–1378

Mons

Wat Phu

Chams

Vijaya

U Thong

Ayutthaya

Rat Buri

Nakhom Pathom

Angkor

Sambor

Andaman
Islands

DVARAVATI
c.550–1050

Tonle Sap

Khmers

Panduranga

Tenasserim

Caturmukha
(Phnom Penh)

CHEN-LA
c.400–800

Andaman
Sea

Gulf of
Thailand

Angkor Borei

Andamanese hunter-gatherers

from India

Chaiya

Ligor

Nicobar
Islands

Sathing Plara

Kedah

Lamri

1295

Samudra
(Pasai)

SAMUDRA
from c.1300

Acehnese

Perlak

1290

Kota Cina

Bataks

Simeulue

Barus

1414

Malacca

Malays

Singapore

Santobong

Nias

Padang
Lawas

Muara
Takas

Sumatra

Da

Minangkabaus

Pagarruyung

Siberut

Malayu

Bangka

Srivijaya

Belitung

Java

1520

Bantam

1500

Sunda

Java

Demak

C

Pajajaran

Borobudur

Dai

Javar

Ked

INDIAN
OCEAN

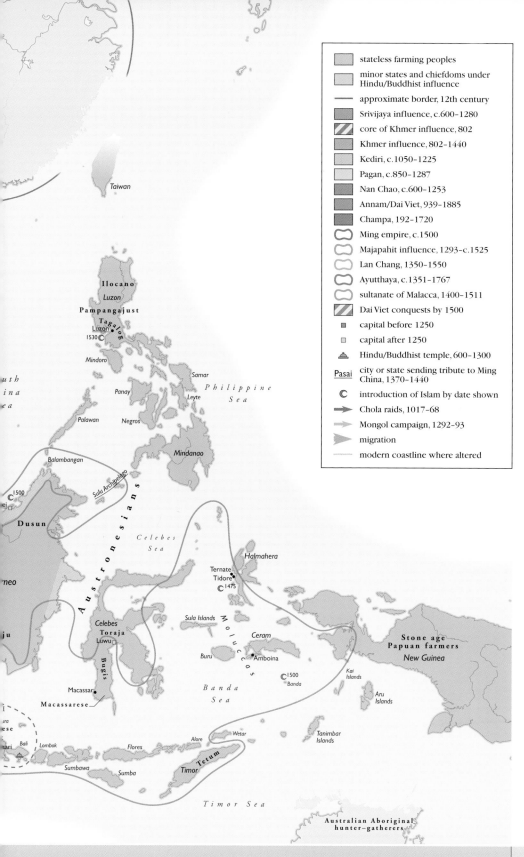

stateless farming peoples

minor states and chiefdoms under Hindu/Buddhist influence

—— approximate border, 12th century

Srivijaya influence, c.600–1280

core of Khmer influence, 802

Khmer influence, 802–1440

Kediri, c.1050–1225

Pagan, c.850–1287

Nan Chao, c.600–1253

Annam/Dai Viet, 939–1885

Champa, 192–1720

Ming empire, c.1500

Majapahit influence, 1293–c.1525

Lan Chang, 1350–1550

Ayutthaya, c.1351–1767

sultanate of Malacca, 1400–1511

Dai Viet conquests by 1500

▪ capital before 1250

▫ capital after 1250

▲ Hindu/Buddhist temple, 600–1300

Pasai   city or state sending tribute to Ming China, 1370–1440

Ⅽ introduction of Islam by date shown

➡ Chola raids, 1017–68

➡ Mongol campaign, 1292–93

▶ migration

—— modern coastline where altered

Taiwan

Ilocano

Luzon

Pampanga just

Tagalog
Luzon
1530 Ⅽ

Mindoro

Samar

Panay

Leyte

Philippine Sea

Palawan

Negros

uth ina a

Mindanao

Balambangan

Sulu Archipelago

1500
Ⅽ
ei

Dusun

A u s t r o n e s i a n s

Celebes Sea

neo

Celebes
Toraja
Luwu

Bugis

Macassar

Macassarese

Halmahera

Ternate
Tidore
Ⅽ 1475

Sula Islands

M o l u c c a s

Ceram

Buru

Amboina

Kai Islands

Ⅽ 1500
Banda

Banda Sea

Aru Islands

Stone age
Papuan farmers
New Guinea

ura ese

sari

Bali

Lombok

Flores

Sumbawa

Sumba

Alore

Wetar

Tetum

Timor

Tanimbar Islands

Timor Sea

Australian Aboriginal
hunter–gatherers

Kingdoms of Southeast Asia

Several small and unstable states arose in mainland and island southeast Asia during the first half of the first millennium CE. By 1000, many stable kingdoms and large empires had emerged. Local rulers, influenced by India, consolidated their power by adopting Buddhist and Hindu concepts of sacred kingship: most southeast Asian states before 1500 were royal theocracies.

Indian cultural influences remained strong throughout the period; China, despite close trade and diplomatic links with some southeast Asian states, only exerted influence on states bordering on it.

The Khmer empire

The most powerful mainland state for much of this period was the Khmer empire of Cambodia. The Khmers had been united in the state of Chen-la around 400 CE. Chen-la peaked in about 700 but soon declined. In 802, Jayavarman II, a minor king in the Angkor district, proclaimed himself *devaraja* ("god-king"), reuniting the Khmer peoples. By 877, the Khmer ruled the Mon and Thai peoples to the north and west. Yasovarman I (r.889– 910) founded a new capital at Angkor, the Khmer empire's most impressive monument. The empire was at its height under Suryavarman I (r.1010–50) and Suryavarman II (r.1113–50). Under pressure from the expanding Thai peoples and the pull of maritime commerce, the Khmer capital moved to the safer location of Caturmukha in 1431 and abandoned Angkor in 1440.

Thai states

The earliest Thai state, the warlike Nan Chao, emerged in about 600; it was finally conquered by the Mongols in 1253. From about 1000, Thai peoples began moving south into Mon and Khmer territories. Powerful kingdoms were established at Sukhothai around 1250 and at Ayutthaya a century later. Ayutthaya conquered Sukhothai in about 1378 and became the dominant power of the Gulf of Thailand by the 15th century after driving the Khmers from Angkor.

The Irrawaddy valley
About 600, Buddhist states began to form among the Mon and Pyu peoples of the Irrawaddy valley. The Pyu states were destroyed by Nan Chao about 835; shortly after, the Burmese moved into the valley and built a state around Pagan. By the mid-11th century, Pagan had created the first unified state in the Irrawaddy basin. It was eventually destroyed by the Mongols.

Dai Viet
Vietnam had been occupied by the Chinese since the third century BCE. In 939, after centuries of rebellion, the Vietnamese founded an independent state, known to them as Dai Viet and to the Chinese as Annam.

Island southeast Asia
The first large state to dominate the sea passages was Srivijaya, in Sumatra. Srivijaya began its imperial expansion in 682 and reached its peak in 800. Raids by the Cholas of south India in the 11th century eroded its power, but its demise was hastened in the first quarter of the 13th century by the imperial expansion of the east Javan Singhasari dynasty. This was in turn succeeded by a new dynasty at Majapahit in 1293. For the next century, Majapahit dominated maritime Indonesia but was in decline by 1400. Only central and east Java was under its direct control, while provincial rulers retained power locally.

Islam, which was brought to island southeast Asia by Indian Muslim merchants at the end of the 13th century, undermined theocratic kingship, founded coastal states, and defeated the remnants of Hindu–Buddhist Majapahit by 1527.

Curriculum Context

Using data in historical maps helps students explain the commercial importance of the Straits of Melaka and the significance of the empire of Srivijaya for maritime trade between China and the Indian Ocean.

Native Cultures of North America

During the period 600 to 1500 CE, farming methods became more productive and the first towns were built in North America.

Siberian hunter–gatherers

Siberian Inuit

Siberian Inuit

Utqiaġ
Birnick
Point Barro
AD 1000
AD 100
Kavik

Uelen
Ekven Cape
Krusenstern
AD 1000
Kungitavik
St Lawrence
Island
Okvik Ahteut
Island Cape Nome
AD 1000
Cape
Denbigh
Yukon

*B e r i n g
S e a*

Nunivak
Island Hooper Bay

AD 1000

Togiak
Beluga Point
Naknek C
Chaluka
Port Moller

COAST

Kodiak
Island

Aleutian Islands

*G u l f   o f
A l a s k a* Glacier Bay

Dodge Islan
*Queen
Charlotte
Islands*

Va

N

Sa

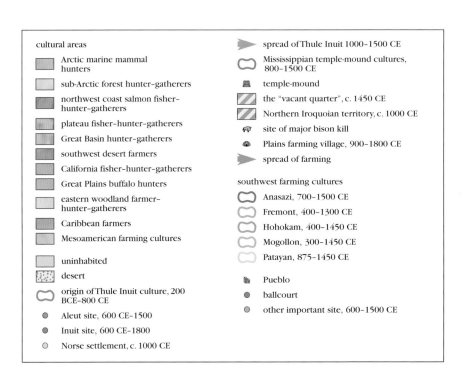

cultural areas

Arctic marine mammal hunters

sub-Arctic forest hunter-gatherers

northwest coast salmon fisher-hunter-gatherers

plateau fisher-hunter-gatherers

Great Basin hunter-gatherers

southwest desert farmers

California fisher-hunter-gatherers

Great Plains buffalo hunters

eastern woodland farmer-hunter-gatherers

Caribbean farmers

Mesoamerican farming cultures

uninhabited

desert

origin of Thule Inuit culture, 200 BCE–800 CE

- Aleut site, 600 CE–1500
- Inuit site, 600 CE–1800
- Norse settlement, c. 1000 CE

spread of Thule Inuit 1000–1500 CE

Mississippian temple-mound cultures, 800–1500 CE

temple-mound

the "vacant quarter", c. 1450 CE

Northern Iroquoian territory, c. 1000 CE

site of major bison kill

Plains farming village, 900–1800 CE

spread of farming

southwest farming cultures

Anasazi, 700–1500 CE

Fremont, 400–1300 CE

Hohokam, 400–1450 CE

Mogollon, 300–1450 CE

Patayan, 875–1450 CE

- Pueblo
- ballcourt
- other important site, 600–1500 CE

P A C
O C

Greenland

Ellesmere
Island

Flagler Bay
Inuarfissuaq
Thule
Illummersuit

Inussuk

Sermermiut

AD 1200–1500

Craig Harbour

Bathurst
Island
Devon Island
Melville
Island
de Blicquy
Maxwell Bay
Nunguvik
Resolute
Strathcona
Sound

AD 1000–1200
Prince of
Wales
Island

Western
Settlement
Illutalik
Kangeq
Eastern
Settlement
Middle
Settlement

Banks
Island

Jackson

Kuujja
Memorana
Victoria
Island
Bell
Pembroke
Clark
Maleruakik

Pingitkalik

AD 1000–1200

Crystal II

L a b r a d o r
S e a

Lady Franklin
Point

Naujan

Baffin Island

Southampton
Island

Silumiut
Igluligardjuk

L'Anse aux
Meadows

Great Bear
Lake

H u d s o n
B a y

Mackenzie

Frank Channel
Great Slave
Lake

Newfoundland
Indian
Point

Charlot River
Lake Athabasca
Reindeer
Lake

Peace

Athabasca

Mingan

Metabetchouan

Saskatchewan

Tailrace Bay
Lake
Winnipeg

Godard Point

Nesikep

Old Women's
Buffalo Jump
Head-Smashed-In

Avonlea

Lake
Superior
Lake
Huron
Lake
Ontario
Maxon-Derby
Nodwell
Sackett

R O C K Y   M O U N T A I N S

Big Hidatsa
Molander
Missouri
Vore
Arzberger

Lake Michigan

St. Lawrence

APPALACHIAN MTS

A T L A N T I C
O C E A N

Columbia

ko River

Wakemap
Mound

Snake

Hogup Cave

Great Plains

Mississippi

Lake
Erie

Big Goose
Creek
Glenrock

Oneota

Proctorville

Wardell

Medicine
Creek

Platte

Arkansas

Old Fort
Cahokia
Angel
Kings Mound
Shiloh

Fort Ancient
Clay Mound

Town Creek
Hiwassee Island
Etowah

Prairie

SIERRA NEVADA

Alkali Ridge
Mesa Verde
Pueblo Bonito
Salmon Ruin
Pecos Pueblo
Chaco
Canyon

Middle
Mississippian

Lamar

Knapp Mounds
Moundville
South Appalachian
Mississippian

Canyon de Chelly
Montezuma
Castle
Mogollon
Topoc Maze

Caddoan

Winterville
Lake Jackson

Pueblo Grande
Snaketown
Casa
Grande
Mimbres
Valley
Garnsey

Plaquemine
Emerald Mound
Mississippian
Coles Creek

Safety Harbor

Casas Grandes

Rio Grande

G u l f   o f
M e x i c o

La Candelaria

Cuba

Native Cultures of North America

The initial settlement of North America began around 12,000 years ago, as bands of Paleo-Indians, the ancestors of modern Native Americans, spread south from Alaska. Adaptation to particular environments led to the emergence of well-defined regional cultures by the end of the first millennium BCE.

From early times, hunter–gatherers in many areas of North America had cultivated favored food plants on a small scale. Some native plant species, such as sunflowers, had been domesticated by the end of the first millennium BCE, and maize and beans had been introduced from Mexico.

Millennium
A period of 1,000 years.

Agriculture and irrigation
The first mainly agricultural North American societies developed in the southwestern deserts in about 300 CE. Maize, beans, squash, and cotton were first cultivated close to permanent water sources but by about 900, elaborate irrigation systems were in use. By the ninth century, three main cultural traditions had developed—the Hohokam, Mogollon, and Anasazi—together with two subsidiary cultures, the Patayan and the Fremont. Their most distinctive remains are their pueblos (multiroomed dwellings) and fine pottery. Droughts caused their decline from around 1300.

Mississippi cultures
True farming began to emerge in the eastern woodlands once hardier strains of maize and beans appeared after 700. The resulting growth in food production stimulated the rise of North America's first towns, in the Mississippi basin, by the 12th century. These centered around large earthwork temple mounds. The Mississippian cultures shared a common religion known as the Southern Cult. Their rulers were buried in mound-top mortuaries with rich grave goods

Mortuaries
Places where dead bodies are kept.

and even human sacrifices. Large Mississippian towns, such as Cahokia, Illinois, were centers of powerful chiefdoms. By the 15th century, Mississippian culture was declining, and its heartland was depopulated. By about 1000, permanent farming villages were established across the eastern woodlands. By the time of European contact, defensive tribal confederacies, such as the Iroquois league, were forming.

Hunters, fishers, and gatherers

Elsewhere in North America, hunting, fishing, and gathering remained the dominant way of life. On the Pacific coast, ocean resources were so abundant that dense populations and permanent village settlements emerged with a high level of social and cultural complexity. The Great Plains and the subarctic forests were sparsely populated, although the advent of the bow and arrow in the first millennium CE made big-game hunting more efficient. At the time of European contact, buffalo hunting was giving way to farming, but the introduction of the horse led many settled Plains peoples to abandon farming for nomadism.

Curriculum Context

Explaining the major characteristics of Anasazi pueblo builders and North American mound-building peoples helps students compare and contrast differing values and institutions.

The Thule Inuit

Arctic North America was uninhabited until about 2500–1900 BCE, when the ancestors of the modern Inuit peoples arrived in Alaska from Siberia. Early Inuit cultures became increasingly well-adapted to the Arctic environment, culminating in the Thule tradition. This originated during the Old Bering Sea Stage (200 BCE–800 CE) among specialized marine mammal hunters on St Lawrence and other Bering Sea islands and spread along Alaska's west coast and north to Point Barrow. Thule Inuit migrated east until they reached Greenland in the 13th century. Here, they made contact with Norse settlers, with whom they traded and fought. The Norse were not well-adapted to life in the Arctic. By about 1500, their settlements had died out and been occupied by the Thule.

Toltecs and Aztecs

In what is now Mexico, the Toltec state was dominant from the 10th to 12th centuries, followed by the Aztecs in the 15th century.

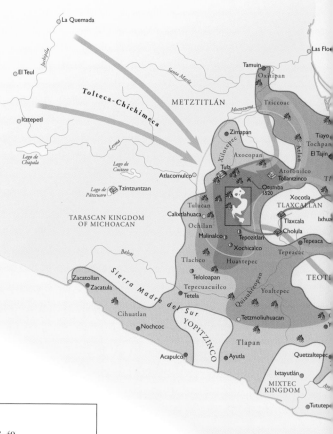

La Quemada

El Teul

Iztepetl

Lago de Chapala

Lago de Cuitzeo

Lago de Pátzcuaro · Tzintzuntzan

TARASCAN KINGDOM OF MICHOACAN

Zacatollan
Zacatula

Sierra Madre del Sur

Cihuatlan

Nochcoc

Acapulco

Balsa

Lerma

Juchipila

Santa María

Tolteca-Chichimeca

METZTITLÁN

Moctezuma

Tamuin

Oxitipan

Tziccoac

Zimapan

Axocopan

Atlacomulco

Tula

Tulucan

Calixtlahuaca

Ochilan

Malinalco

Xochicalco

Tlachco

Tepozitlan

Huaxtepec

Teloloapan

Tepecuacuilco
Tetela

Tetzmoliuhuacan

Tlapan

Ayutla

Tzmoliuhuacan

Quiauheyapan

Yoaltepec

Xilotepec

Atotonilco
Tollantzinco

Otumba
1520

Xocotla
TLAXCALLAN

Tlaxcala

Cholula

Tepeaca

Tepeacac

Las Flor

Tiayo
Tochpan
El Tajin

Ixhua

TEOTI

Quetzaltepec

Ixtayutlán
MIXTEC KINGDOM

Tututepe

Atl

Legend:

- Toltec empire, c.1200
- Aztec empire under Itzcóatl, 1427–40
- expansion under Moctezuma I, 1440–68 and Axayacatl, 1469–81
- expansion under Ahuitzotl, 1486–1502 and Moctezuma II, 1502–20
- late Postclassic Maya states
- borders, c.1520
- major Postclassic Maya site
- other Postclassic Maya site
- major Toltec site
- other Toltec site
- major Aztec site
- other Aztec site
- other major Postclassic site
- other site
- Aztec garrison
- Tlacopán — city of the Triple Alliance
- Putún Maya trade route
- migration, c.900
- Toltec migration, c.980–1200
- route of Cortés, April to November 1519

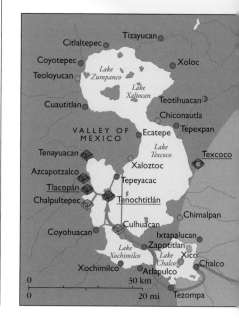

Citlaltepec

Tizayucan

Coyotepec

Teoloyucan

Lake Zumpanco

Lake Xaltocan

Xoloc

Cuautitlan

Teotihuacan

Chiconautla

VALLEY OF MEXICO

Ecatepe

Tepexpan

Tenayuacan

Lake Texcoco

Azcapotzalco

Xaloztoc

Texcoco

Tlacopán

Tepeyacac

Chalpultepec

Tenochtitlán

Culhuacan

Chimalpan

Coyohuacan

Ixtapalucan

Lake Xochimilco

Zapotitlan

Lake Chalco

Xico

Xochimilco

Atlapulco

Chalco

Tezompa

0   30 km

0   20 mi

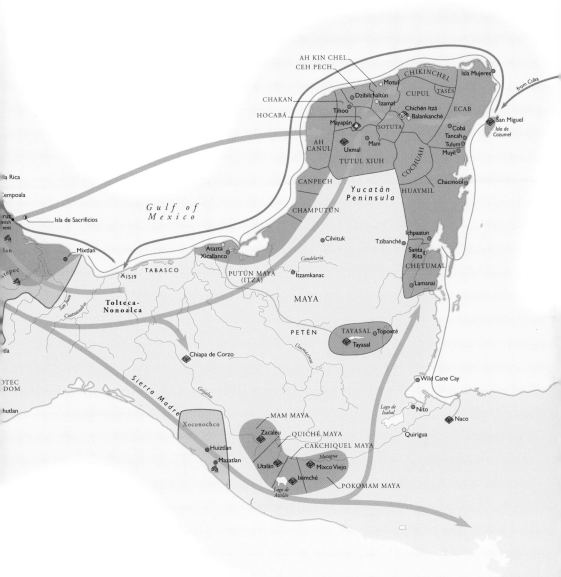

AH KIN CHEL
CEH PECH
CHIKINCHEL
Isla Mujeres
Motul
CUPUL
TASES
CHAKAN
Dzibilchaltún
Izamal
Chichén Itzá
ECAB
HOCABÁ
Tihoo
Balankanché
Mayapán
San Miguel
SOTUTA
Cobá
Isla de
Cozumel
AH
Tancah
CANUL
Uxmal
Mani
Tulum
TUTUL XIUH
COCHUAH
Muyil
CANPECH
Yucatán
Peninsula
HUAYMIL
CHAMPUTÚN
Chacmool

Gulf of
Mexico

Ila Rica
Cempoala

Cilvituk
Ichpaatun
Tzibanché
Santa
Rita
CHETUMAL

ruz
ish
ent
Isla de Sacrificios

Mixtlan
Atazta
Xicallanco
Candelaria
Lamanai

TABASCO
1519
PUTÚN MAYA
(ITZÁ)
Itzamkanac

pec

MAYA

San Juan
Coatzacoalcos

Tolteca-
Nonoalca

PETÉN
TAYASAL
Topoxté
Tayasal

Wild Cane Cay

Chiapa de Corzo

Usumacinta

tla

TEC
DOM

Sierra Madre

Grijalva

Lago de
Izabal
Nito

Quirigua
Naco

hutlan

Xoconochco

MAM MAYA
Zacaleu
QUICHÉ MAYA
CAKCHIQUEL MAYA
Huiztlan
Utalán
Mixco Viejo
Mazatlan
Iximché
Lago de
Atitlán
POKOMAM MAYA

from Cuba

Toltecs and Aztecs

The destruction of Teotihuacán in the eighth century left a power vacuum in central Mexico, which allowed new peoples to migrate to the region. The Chichimeca and the Nonoalca settled to the north of the Valley of Mexico, where they merged to form the Toltec nation. By around 900, a Toltec state was established around Tula, from where it expanded over the Valley of Mexico.

Little is known of the history of the Toltecs, but their legends feature prominently in the traditions of the Aztecs, who claimed descent from them.

The feathered serpent

The most important legend concerns the Toltec ruler Topiltzin-Quetzalcóatl, a real person born in 935 or 947 who soon came to be identified with the god Quetzalcóatl ("feathered serpent"). His opposition to human sacrifice offended the god Tezcatlipoca, who overthrew him. Topiltzin-Quetzalcóatl fled, vowing to return one day to reclaim his kingdom. Mayan records show that in 987 a man called Kukulcán ("feathered serpent" in Mayan) conquered Yucatán. Archeological evidence confirms that in about 1000 the Mayan city of Chichén Itzá was occupied by Toltecs.

The Aztec empire

Tula was sacked in about 1168, and the Toltec empire was supplanted by many rival city-states. Around 1200, the Aztecs, a farming people from the west, moved into the Valley of Mexico, eventually founding a permanent settlement at Tenochtitlán in 1325. First serving as mercenaries for Tezozomoc, ruler of Azcapotzalco, the Aztecs allied with Texcoco to destroy Azcapotzalco after Tezozomoc's death in 1426. Two years later, Itzcóatl established a strong Aztec monarchy. In 1434, Tenochtitlán, Texcoco, and Tlacopan formed the Triple Alliance, imposing tributary status on

Mercenaries
Hired soldiers.

the other states of the Valley of Mexico. By 1500, the alliance ruled over some 10 million people. The empire peaked under Moctezuma II (r.1502–20) but was abruptly ended by Hernán Cortés' invasion of 1519–21. Although Cortés had great advantages in weaponry and armor, the Aztecs had overwhelming superiority of numbers. Moctezuma vacillated, believing Cortés to be the returning Quetzalcóatl, whom the legends described as fair-skinned and bearded. The Mesoamerican custom of taking prisoners for sacrifice also hampered the Aztecs against the conquistadors, who fought to kill. Cortés found willing allies in the Tlaxcallans, the Aztecs' main source of sacrificial victims. Finally, diseases brought by the Spanish, such as smallpox, decimated the Aztecs.

Curriculum Context

Many curricula ask students to analyze how the Aztec empire arose in the 14th and 15th centuries and explain major aspects of Aztec government, society, religion, and culture.

Conquistador

A Spanish conqueror of Central and South America in the 16th century.

Aztec society

At the time of the conquest, Aztec society was a class-based hierarchy. Relatives of the king formed the aristocracy, while the commoners comprised members of 20 clans. Each clan had its own quarter of the city with its own schools, temples, and communal farms. The lowest class were conquered peoples, who served the aristocracy as farmers and laborers. There were also slaves—usually war captives—and a merchant class.

Maya states

After the Classic Maya cities of the Petén lowlands were abandoned in about 800, Mayan civilization continued in northern Yucatán. Around 850–900 the Putún, or Itza Maya, settled at Chichén Itzá, which quickly became the dominant Maya center. Around 1000, Yucatán was conquered by the Toltecs, whose rule ended in 1221 with the fall of Chichén Itzá to Hunac Ceel, ruler of Mayapán. The Cocom dynasty he founded dominated Yucatán for over 200 years. When the Spanish landed on Yucatán in 1517, the northern Maya were divided into 16 rival states. Tayasal, the last independent Maya state, did not fall until 1697.

Andean Civilizations

In the Andean region, many states, large and small, formed after 1000 CE, before the Incans created a vast highland and coastal empire in the 15th century.

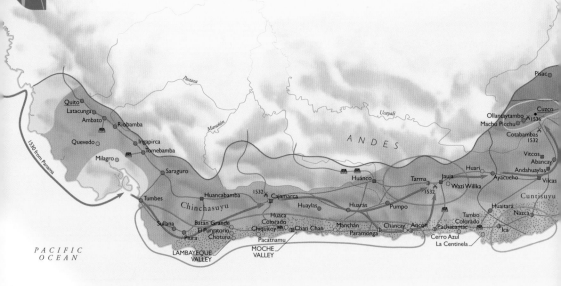

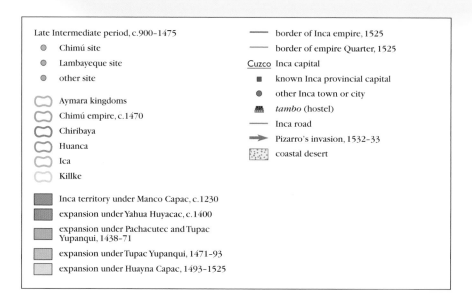

Late Intermediate period, c.900–1475		border of Inca empire, 1525
●	Chimú site	border of empire Quarter, 1525
●	Lambayeque site	Cuzco Inca capital
●	other site	■ known Inca provincial capital
		● other Inca town or city
	Aymara kingdoms	🏯 *tambo* (hostel)
	Chimú empire, c.1470	Inca road
	Chiribaya	➤ Pizarro's invasion, 1532–33
	Huanca	coastal desert
	Ica	
	Killke	

Inca territory under Manco Capac, c.1230

expansion under Yahua Huyacac, c.1400

expansion under Pachacutec and Tupac Yupanqui, 1438–71

expansion under Tupac Yupanqui, 1471–93

expansion under Huayna Capac, 1493–1525

Hualla
Tampu

Cochabamba

Antisuyu

Paria

La Paz

Lake Titicaca

Tiahuanaco

*Lake
Poopó*

Tupiza

Ayaviri

ncolla

Chucuito

Huamachuco

Tilcara

tani

Alto Ramirez

Collasuyu

Mt Acay

La Playa

Chiribaya Alto

Pica

Santa Maria

Catarpe

Pucara de
Andalgala

San Pedro
de Atacama

Belén

Chilecito

Copiapo

A N D E S

Ranchillos

Santiago

Talca

Andean Civilizations

The collapse of the highland Tiahuanaco and Huari empires in about 1000 ushered in a long period of political fragmentation in the Andean civilizations. Both in the highlands and on the coast, many local states emerged. Most of them, like the Sicán state of Lambayeque, controlled no more than a single valley.

Around 1200, the Chimú state, centered on Chan Chan in the Moche valley, began a period of expansion. In the 15th century, it controlled over 620 miles (1,000 km) of the Peruvian coast. In the early 13th century, Manco Capac founded the Inca state at Cuzco in the Killke area of the highlands. For a long time, the Inca state controlled little more than the valley around Cuzco but in the 15th century, it became the greatest of all the empires of the pre-Columbian Americas.

Inca expansion and decline

At its peak in around 1500, the Inca empire encompassed much of modern Peru and Bolivia, together with sizable portions of Chile, Argentina, and Equador, and ruled over some 12 million people. The Incas' remarkable territorial expansion took place almost entirely during the reigns of Pachacutec (r.1438–71) and Tupac Yupanqui (r.1471–93). The Incas overcame the Chimú with little difficulty, capturing their capital Chan Chan in 1470. Territorial gains were made in the north under Huayna Capac (r. 1493–1525) but on his death, a bloody civil war broke out between his sons Atahuallpa and Huáscar. Atahuallpa finally triumphed in 1532, but he had no opportunity to restore the weakened empire. In the same year, the Spanish conquistador Francisco Pizarro invaded and captured Atahuallpa. In 1533, the Spanish executed Atahuallpa and installed a puppet ruler at Cuzco: When he rebelled in 1536, they assumed direct rule. Inca resistance was finally crushed in 1572.

Curriculum Context

Many curricula ask students to analyze Inca expansion and methods of imperial unification.

Puppet ruler

A ruler who is controlled by influences outside the state.

Inca military strategy

Inca nobles were brought up in the arts of war, and a standing army was maintained, so the empire was able to react quickly to any threat. The Incas built a network of roads around 12,500 miles (20,000 km) long, which allowed troops to move quickly to quell trouble on the borders or in the provinces. Rebels were deported to the heart of the empire, where they could be supervised; their lands were settled by loyal Incas.

Inca administration

Inca society was highly centralized and rigidly hierarchical. Below the emperor, and directly answerable to him, were the prefects of the Four Quarters, and below them provincial governors, followed by district officers, local chiefs, and, at the bottom, foremen who were each responsible for supervising 10 families. Farmland was divided into thirds, for the support of the state, the gods, and the people respectively.

Curriculum Context

Comparing the government, economy, religion, and social organization of the Aztec and Inca empires is an exercise in comparing and contrasting differing values and institutions.

Inca taxes

All Inca men and women contributed taxation in the form of labor on those parts of the land allocated to the state and the gods. Able-bodied men also paid tax through a labor draft known as *mit'a*. This could last for months and range from military service to work on major construction projects, such as roads and fortresses, or agricultural improvements, such as terracing steep hillsides in order to grow more crops. This tax system enabled the Inca empire to raise and supply large armies and keep them in the field for long campaigns.

Reasons for defeat

Although the long and destructive civil war coincided with Pizarro's invasion, the centralized hierarchy of the Inca empire was also partly responsible for its swift demise. No major decision could be taken without the emperor, so the empire was paralyzed once Atahuallpa had been captured.

Glossary

Annexed Incorporated within another state.

Aristocracy A small, privileged minority with great influence in government.

Bureaucracy A government with fixed rules, specialized functions and a clear hierarchy of authority.

Caliphate The territory ruled by a caliph, who was the spiritual and earthly head of Islam.

Canton A small territorial division of a country.

Caste A social class with its own occupations and restrictions.

Claimant Someone who asserts a right to a title or a territory.

Clan A group of people with a common ancestor.

Composite bow A bow made of horn, sinew, and wood that is smaller and more powerful than an all-wood bow.

Confederation An alliance.

Confucianism An ethical and philosophical system developed from the teachings of Chinese philosopher Confucius (551–479 BCE) that became influential in Eastern Asia.

Conquistador A Spanish conqueror of Central and South America in the 16th century.

Duchy The territory ruled by a duke.

Emirate A state ruled by an Islamic chief known as an emir.

Exarchate A region ruled by an exarch, who was a Byzantine viceroy.

Fee A feudal estate.

Hegemony Influence or authority over others.

Hinterland A region beyond an urban center.

Historiography Writing about history.

Khandom State ruled by a khan.

Martyrdom Suffering death for one's religious faith.

Mercantile Relating to trade or merchants.

Mercenaries Hired soldiers.

Monophysite Believing that Christ's nature is inseparably divine and human, rather than consisting of two distinct natures.

Monotheism The belief that there is only one god.

Oligarchy A government controlled by a small group of people.

Orthodox Christianity A form of Christianity that follows traditional Greek rites.

Papacy The system of government of the Roman Catholic church, headed by the pope.

Penance An act to show repentance for sin.

Protectorate A state that is dependent on or under the authority of another.

Puppet ruler A ruler who is controlled by influences outside the state.

Regency Government by a person or persons while a sovereign is too young or disabled to govern or in the absence of the sovereign.

Schism A division within a religious body.

Secede To withdraw from a state or an organization.

See The region containing a cathedral, over which a bishop has power.

Serfdom The state of being a serf, having to work on the land and be subject to the will of the land's owner.

Shahdom A territory ruled by a shah in Greater Iran (an area including modern Iran, Turkmenistan, and Uzbekistan, and parts of Afghanistan, Kazakhstan, Tajikistan, and Kyrgyzstan).

Shamanism A religion in which spirits of gods or ancestors are contacted by shamans, who are priests and diviners.

Shogunate A Japanese state under military government, led by a shogun.

Silk Road A network of trade routes across Asia, connecting China, India, Persia, and West Asia with the Mediterranean. They were originally created for the Chinese silk trade.

Sub-Saharan Describes the part of Africa south of the Sahara.

Teutonic Knights A German Roman Catholic religious and military order that organized crusades in northern Europe against the non-Christian Baltic Prussians and Lithuanians.

Theocratic Governed by people who are guided by a god or by divine beings.

Tribute Payment by one state to another for protection or to indicate submission.

Vassal A person who swears to obey a lord in return for protection.

Further Research

BOOKS

Bishop, Morris. *The Middle Ages*. Mariner Books, 2001.

Coe, Michael D., and Rex Koontz. *Mexico: From the Olmecs to the Aztecs*. Thames & Hudson, 2008.

Cook, William R., and Ronald B. Herzman. *The Medieval World View: An Introduction*. Oxford University Press, 2003.

D'Altroy, Terence N. *The Incas*. Wiley-Blackwell, 2003.

Ebrey, Patricia Buckley. *The Cambridge Illustrated History of China*. Cambridge University Press, 1999.

Ehret, Christopher. *The Civilizations of Africa: A History to 1800*. University of Virginia Press, 2002.

Gregory, Timothy. *A History of Byzantium*. Wiley-Blackwell, 2005.

Haywood, John. *The Penguin Historical Atlas of the Vikings*. Penguin, 1995.

Holmes, George, ed. *The Oxford Illustrated History of Medieval Europe*. Oxford University Press, USA, 2001.

Inalcik, Halil. *The Ottoman Empire: The Classical Age 1300–1600*. Phoenix, 2001.

Johansen, Bruce E. *The Native Peoples of North America: A History*. Rutgers University Press, 2006.

Keay, John. *India: A History*. Grove Press, 2001.

Madden, Thomas F. *Crusades: The Illustrated History*. University of Michigan Press, 2005.

Newman, Paul B. *Daily Life in the Middle Ages*. McFarland, 2001.

Saunders, J. J. *The History of the Mongol Conquests*. University of Pennsylvania Press, 2001.

Sider, Sandra. *Handbook to Life in Renaissance Europe*. Oxford University Press, USA, 2007.

Sonn, Tamara. *A Brief History of Islam*. Wiley-Blackwell, 2004.

Tarling, Nicholas, ed. *The Cambridge History of Southeast Asia*. Cambridge University Press, 2000.

Totman, Conrad. *A History of Japan*. Wiley-Blackwell, 2005.

INTERNET RESOURCES

History of China. This website includes articles on all the Chinese dynasties with maps and illustrations.
www.history-of-china.com

EMuseum@Minnesota State University. The Prehistory section includes the cultures of North America, Mesoamerica, and South America. The History section has much information on the Anglo-Saxons, medieval Europe, Russia, China, Japan, and the Silk Road.
www.mnsu.edu/emuseum

The End of Europe's Middle Ages: Fourteenth & Fifteenth Centuries. A summary of the economic, political, religious, and intellectual environment of the time.
www.ucalgary.ca/applied_history/tutor/endmiddle

International World History Project. A collection of essays, documents, and maps on world history.
www.history-world.org

The Islamic World to 1600. This website includes five chapters of detailed Islamic history and one of arts and learning.
www.ucalgary.ca/applied_history/tutor/islam

Macrohistory and World Report. This site contains detailed information in the section Middle Ages, the World from the 6th to 15th Centuries.
www.fsmitha.com/h3/index.htm

Neobyzantine. A detailed site about the Byzantine world and empire.
www.neobyzantine.org

TheOttomans.org. A detailed history of the Ottomans, century by century.
www.theottomans.org/english/history/index.asp

The Story of Africa: African History from the Dawn of Time. A comprehensive history of the continent.
www.bbc.co.uk/worldservice/specials/1624_story_of_africa/index.shtml

Index